MANAGING

A

CHRISTIAN

WORLD

David O. Okoduwa

ISBN: 978-978-957-335-6

Printed in Lagos, Nigeria.

.

PUBLISHED BY:
Wisdom Literary & Management Agency
25, Adefimihan Street,
Off Mushin-Itire Road,
Lagos, Nigeria.
Tel: +2348089657685, +2348098745556
Email: wisdomliterary@gmail.com

CONTENTS

FOREWORD

Managing A Christian World is a book prompting Christianity lifestyle; and studying this book, my discovery is that you can live in the world not as a Christian; but saying that you are a Christian then you have to adhere to the Lord Jesus' words: *"these words spake Jesus, and lifted up his eyes to heaven, and said, Father, the hour is come; glorify thy Son, that thy Son also may glorify thee: as thou hast given him power over all flesh, that he should give eternal life to as many as thou hast given him,* (John 17:2-3). That's exactly is the picture!

And this Christian book has shown much of your lifestyle and also an opening for you to know who you are. Our Lord Jesus makes us to understand the principles of life as a Christian, "…what Jesus began to do and teach," (Acts 1:1). *Managing A Christian World* teaches us how to live in the world undergoing corruption without being corrupt, as the Bible says: Love not the world neither the things that are in the world: for if any one loves the world then the love of God is not in him; all that is in this world is lust, (1John 2:15-17).

This book will teach you how you will have supernatural power to overcome the world we are in today because the world is full of evil. You can only become saved if you are in Christ Jesus and then have peace in the world. There are vices of evil to subdue but you need God in this wicked world and through this book, understanding will come.

The book talks about the grace for realities because we need the grace of God to perform all our activities on earth, and as strangers in this world, God is all we need. We need supernatural influence which is what this book is encouraging us to know and be able to take the world in our hands - knowing the time, and that now is the high time to awake to realities; for the time is far spent, (Romans 13:11)..

As Christians, we need to believe God because the unbelievers do not have part in this book prepared for God's people, except that they wish to take part, (1 Peter 2:9). You are a chosen generation, a royal priesthood, a holy nation, a peculiar people, that you should show forth the glory of God.

Whosoever will not manage his life aright in the eyes of God will end up in the Hell fire. I read the book brethren, apprehensive of the Author's views and also his testimony, then I understand that we need to manage our lives well in the midst of crooked people, where now spiritual nakedness is nothing before the people of this world, (Exodus 33:12-14).

Reading this book will remind you who you are and make you focus. I recommend this book: *Managing A Christian World* to you; read this book and remain a holy Christian as we run the race of heaven.

Pastor John Mbah

INTRODUCTION

We live in a world broken into fragments by religions! Attitude reveals a lot about various religion followers, Christianity inclusive. In a way, we have a world meshed of characters because of religion; but who is identified? You and I are identified by certain percentage of religious behaviour which presents to people around us who we are and what religion we profess. On this ground this book is written.

Basing on Christians' attitude in our time, it's more of assignments to preview and also review what our Lord Jesus Christ actually meant when he said: *they are not of the world, even as I am not of the world. Sanctify them through thy truth: thy word is truth. As thou has sent me into the world, even so have I also sent them into the world,*" *(John 17:16-18).*

Haven't we got a pattern to mirror our attitude here on earth? Do we have to water down so great settings that we may walk on our own ways forward? Or have we ignored his words for our choices to stay? Now we got a world at hand that's troubled by having God's creation in the wilfulness of men like in the days of Noah when men sunk in sinful attitude were eating and drinking, marrying and giving away in marriage until destruction came upon them. Then I knew something unknown to many and I chose to draw them out in this work that we may altogether adjust our attitude to fashion for selves a Christian world; so personal in reviewing your lifestyles and at the same time helpful in growing one's spiritual life in all Christian ways.

Considering we have a duty on earth to eschew evil, some unspiritual acts we exhibit daily are dealt with to enable us achieve victory over the enemies. We need spiritual strength in all areas, whether be it close or distant matters; ghostly or physical – knowing that there are purposes why we live; if not for material blessings, let it be for spiritual endowments.

Christians are getting weaker in exploiting their place on

earth, because of introductions of sensational projects, elations, behaviours, sentiments, craftiness, etc. We keep warring in flesh, and in *prayer*; but have we given our thoughts to dwell on the numbers of people derailed by lies and presence of agents of darkness operating within the church walls?

If vices of evil must be subdued in your lifetime to bring his glorious grace upon your days, be quicken by all matters addressed in this book: '*Managing a Christian World*'. You can't hide from being a Christian, whether when you do well in attitude or when you fail in it; knowing that people are seeing your involvement whether scarcely or committedly and also that the LORD God is faithful to man even in his weakness.

What about his grace for realities? When we haply failed, he still cares. But one thing is sure that we are indebted to righteousness all the way as Christians. To say that the world is waiting for the manifestation of the sons of God is not saying the world is waiting for the numbers of people who profess Christianity, but for the weight of righteousness which must cover the earth as the waters cover the sea, (Isaiah 11:1-10). That's what the world of men has not experienced!

Righteousness is wearing away from the earth as waters dried from the sea because of fickle practice of it since lies are much and errors prosper from the churches on earth. If you must count yourself out, read this book!

David O. Okoduwa
(Gifted-healer)

Chapter One

A CHRISTIAN'S WORLD

We are transiting out from what we see today as our world into eternity. Therefore let us live out our lives within the proclaimed Salvation through Jesus Christ that actually entails our commitment to the things of God which are based on Christ principles, (Luke 14:25-35).

In wisdom, avoidance of God's wrath must have a place in all of us. If you say you are a child of God, know Jesus by principles of **appearance, clothing, fellowship, and self-structured world.**

Passion for the things that surround you is likely to be passion for the hollow around you. If you must build a kingdom within you; better to form that kingdom within that represents the purpose of Christ on earth (whether be you a preacher of the gospel of Christ or a believer in Christ,) we all are called for same purpose, (Jeremiah 1:16; 17:13; 9:13-16).

Remember this always; that the love from Satan towards any person is done to give him or her all what he or she wants at all times; but the love of God gives you what you need at a time, leading you to enjoy a peaceful time. God did not tell anyone to live complaining for earthly things but that one lives taking over the world of men to subdue it unto Christ Jesus our Lord, (Romans 8:17-31; Phil. 4:4-8).

Basically, our lives are weighed on this wise:

"For the wrath of God is revealed from heaven against all ungodliness and unrighteousness of men, who hold the truth in unrighteousness; because that which may be known about God is manifest in them; for God hath shewed it unto them. For the invisible things of him

from the creation of the world are clearly seen, being understood by the things that are made, even his eternal power and Godhead; so that they are without excuse: **because that when they knew God, they glorified him not as God,** *neither were they thankful; but became vain in their imaginations, and their foolish heart was darkened". (Romans 1:18-21).*

Take a quick reasoning from a man that does things being projected with his shadow image. Functionally, what he does is exactly what his shadow is at the same time doing. The shadow is acting together in conformity with the man who has it; for the shadow itself is drawn from him. But there is a third person also in action doing like he and the shadow do. That is his spiritual person! The man might see and think about his shadow, but of his spiritual person not a thought is offered.

Life should not be seen only of the flesh. Though a man's spiritual self is hidden because of his ignorance, what helps a man to have spiritual gains or losses is his spiritual self. His spiritual self is the peace or trouble he would experience in his lifetime. If he lived uprightly unto God and man, his spiritual self gained momentum in empowerment to conquer and overcome in all things, (2 Cor. 8:21). If he otherwise lived unto himself in errors of sin, his spiritual self had done sin, and his shadow also was involved as he must have seen his shadow doing what he was doing.

If we say his shadow has no responsibility but his spiritual self do have responsibility in all that the man has given himself to do. Your spiritual self is weak when you are sinful. You can be taken captive and be destroyed by the evildoers who operate in the spiritual world, (Read Prov. 4:14-18). Science may not accept this, but one thing is true; science is the voice and revealer of secret things. All sufferings a man goes through in his body are not all quite ordinary; some are spiritual, (Ephesians 6:12).

A Christian can develop himself and create an overcomer's world for himself. Better to be empowered to over-

9

throw the wickedness in spiritual places than to pursue to gain the pleasures of earthly things. Take time to read Matthew 6:19-32 and Jeremiah 1:1-10. Being a Christian is being a god in the earth and a Christian is being represented in the spiritual world by his spiritual self which he is expected to accountably present to the world of men in spiritual behaviour, (Read Psalm 82:1-6; John 10:33-36; 2Corithians 6:14-18).Therefore be led to defend and manage a Christian's world thus:

1. Appearance:

A person's appearance affects the spiritual world either negatively or positively; just as his or her shadow shows what he or she is doing so his spiritual self reveals what he or she gives himself to do to the spiritual world where evil abounds more than the person thinks of them in the physical.

Appearance of a man considers the thoughts of his heart. Out of the abundance of the heart he generates a look and countenance which men see of him at all times. His status among others is as a result of what he considers of himself and definitely he cannot hide what he is, in glory or in common nature. I don't think anyone would want to see a pastor among drunkards also drinking beer filled of high alcohol. Then he had rubbished his appearance physically and spiritually though he dressed and talked like a pastor at all times. This will affect his worth in the spiritual world because his spiritual self drank with him and his shadow did too. Obviously his spiritual self and his shadow had no senses to decide their involvement; but while his shadow has no responsibility, his spiritual self got damned in helplessness. The man is becoming a wrong one in the eye of God, and the devil loved that – another seed of damnation!

Therefore, a man's appearance is not to be seen as the clothes he wears, or the appellations to his name, neither is it his fair or ugly look; but the tendencies of keeping and maintaining his spiritual self to defeat what would break into his life and take it over, or tendencies of appearing defeated ever. That which is of the spirit is spirit, and that which is of the flesh is flesh. If a man is not spiritually empowered he is damned and powerless. Always make your appearance reveal the 'you' in you because of your spiritual self. Let your countenance express the Christ resilience and conquering spirit and you will experience His proclaimed Salvation.

Simon Peter, a Christ disciple had lost his appearance at one time. He was called out of his former self as a fisherman to become a fisher of men; and he went along with our Lord Jesus as though he had all realities inside him appearing as a lieutenant of the Master, (Matt. 4:18-20). Peter from inside knew Jesus as the Messiah, and he was prepared to defend Him and deny Him not, (Matt. 16:13-16; 26:31-35). At that time, he bore the countenance that revealed a strong spiritual self. He could be feared and respected for that. Oh yes! He seemed to show the merits.

But deep inside he wasn't actually there for himself to defend his Master in the hours of trials. Then he denied Jesus. And then again he went fishing after Jesus was crucified. His spiritual self took Jesus in the spiritual world in notice to come to the seaside to see his common self labouring again as he used to be with him, (Matt. 26:69-75; John 21:1-7).

And Jesus weighed Peter in his loss of spiritual appearance and said:

"Simon, son of Jonas, lovest thou me more than these? He saith unto him, Yea, Lord: thou knowest that I love thee. He saith unto him: feed my lambs," (John 21:15).

So it is with thousands of Christians today switching off after a period of life sustaining fellowship with God in churches to become the nature the Devil can subdue; because they are not steadfast in Christian appearance. When you meet a lion, should it not be seen in the spirit of a lion which he is? So should a Christian be seen in appearance!

11

"For in him (Jesus) we live, and move, and have our beings..." (Acts 17:28).

Now, I look forward believing in him for somebody who must decide to live for Him, and I can tell God is coming to you with a blessing and a miracle in Jesus name, Amen!!!

2. Clothing:

The place of clothing in a person's life is psychological and it has positive or negative effects on his or her spiritual self, though he or she has no thoughts for that. Clothing oneself is a necessity and very enslaving. Nevertheless, the clothing people are adapted to is their choices borne out of culture, religion, tendency and corporatism. Weighing all these on the balance, the questionable one is the clothing borne out of tendency which is capable of defacing the other patterns of clothing. Tendency is ironic in any thing called clothing: if it does not tell of dignity, it will definitely tell of arrogance or carelessness. Tendency is crafty and dangerous where it does not respect who you should be but rather what you carelessly decide to be. Apostle Paul says in **Hebrews 12:1**.

"Wherefore seeing we also are compassed about with so great a cloud of witnesses, let us lay aside every weight and the sin which doth so easily beset us..."

A believer's world, as a Christian, must be evaluated in the senses of that Christianity spirit which reflects certain features a Christian man or woman must display with respect for them from time to time. Better for a believer in Christ to base clothing assignments on exceptional ground of religion as credibly approved by the system. One's spiritual self suffers reprobation challenges because of what he or she carelessly put on as should be noted that the eyes of people and the spiritual world view the clothing pattern with disdain. I don't suppose anyone will esteem a virgin or a convert sister who tendentiously wore what women from a brothel are seen with and claimed she has a Bible, and a church and a pastor as a defence. If she's in church system, let her posture be included by the eyes that view her composition; for we are called to show forth distinction.

In Joseph's days coat of many colours drew evil to him! As people do not attach value to you in your careless, indecent clothing, so also the spiritual world to your spiritual self: for your spiritual self is marked with clothing whether you agree to this or not. A person is considered reprobate when clothing match contrary to who he or she must be regarded to be. (Read Deut. 22:5; 1Cor. 11:4-12; Eph. 2:10-12; 2Tim. 2:15). Who you are should stand above what you choose to be seen wearing in the eyes of people.

A Christian man adorning himself like the women do has depleted his personality in the spiritual world; although here in the physical it is his fair look, yet in the spiritual world he's reprobate. Apostle Paul says:

"I beseech you therefore, brethren, by the mercies of God, that ye present your bodies a living sacrifice, holy, acceptable unto God, which is your reasonable service. And be not conformed to this world: but be ye transformed by the renewing of your mind, that ye may prove what is that good, and perfect, will of God." *(Romans 12:1-2).*

If there be no spiritual implications cautionary Biblical verses would be of no use for a record. The Law of Moses says:

"The woman shall not wear that which pertaineth unto a man; neither shall a *man put on a woman's garment: for all that do so are abomination unto the LORD thy God." (Deut.22:5).*

13

The word a man tells another man may endure but for a short moment, and the word of God endures forever – no negotiation. To be rated an abominable condemns the spiritual self of a person in the spiritual world. Then he or she cannot escape afflictions from the wicked realms where wickedness in high places is practiced. And when he prays, there is no result; he's an outcast in the eye of God. I would better not let my spiritual self be rejected by God! Therefore let wisdom direct you in this matter. Do not wear that dress because it is wearable or that other people wear such or allow such to be seen on them. A person becomes unique when he or she is a follower of Jesus Christ. **Clothing discipline saves one's spiritual self.**

3. Fellowship:

Fellowship in preview is like mapping the consciousness of a person based on which area his or her consciousness is bound in relatedness or connection. On social ground, think about one's relationship with friends; and on classical ground, think about one's relationship with colleagues of same profession; and on waywardness, think about what a person is drawn into without conscious reasoning and yet he or she is indulgent; and on spiritual ground, think about one's spiritual communion with a divine being.

Fellowship takes the larger part of a person's life because it reveals his or her lifestyle to others. It also has its positive and negative effects on one's spiritual self. And fellowship allows habits. Take note that when habits are generated in a person, he or she is held captive by them – the dangerous part of fellowship! That man around you was not addicted to drugs before now, but one pattern of fellowship caused it when it does develop to habitual level! The other fellow has become more relevant and without questionable character traits, one pattern of fellowship made him so.

14

"Wherefore by their fruits ye shall know them."
(Matthew 7:20).

It is either fellowship makes you or damages you and your spiritual self in the spiritual world and the world of men; but people who know you are not really bothered over your lifestyles when you are satisfied living them out. But, are you really?

"There is a way which seemeth right unto a man, but the end thereof are the ways of death", (Proverbs 14:12).

Even as no man troubles you, not much like your spiritual self does, bringing you out in behavioural despondency against your physical person. When a man adapts mostly to worldly fellowship than that of relatedness unto God, his spiritual self sells him out in all behaviours because the spirits of error have him bound in reprobation. Believe me reader, that man is having crises of demonization. Oh yes! Do not argue!

*"And even as they did not like to retain God in their knowledge, **God gave them over to a reprobate mind, to do those things which are not convenient**; being filled with all unrighteousness, fornication, wickedness, maliciousness; full of envy, murder, debate, deceit, malignity; whisperers...* who *knowing the judgment of God, that they which commit such things are worthy of death, not only do the same, but have pleasure in them that do them." (Romans 1:28-32).*

The nature of man is a host of spirits which actively move him to actions; and when he is not a temple for the Holy Spirit, he must be influenced by other spirits knowingly or unknowingly. Therefore make yourself available for God's fellowship where erratic attitudes to life are checked with the use of the Gospel of

15

Christ Jesus.

"O LORD, I know that the way of man is not in himself: it is not in man that walketh to direct his steps." (Jeremiah 10:23).

Oh dear, if you don't live with this; always seeing God managing your life through fellowship with Him at all times, you are vulnerable to afflictions because your spiritual self is in helplessness: and wicked eyes can lay siege until you fall in grace, wealth and health, (Read Psalms 1:1-6). Deliverance is not always achieved with prayers but with determination to quit self obsession to worldliness. Not until you set yourself free truth won't make you free, (John 8:32).

4. Self-structured World:

This is a self-contained world generated for self in coded appearance, clothing, and fellowship which people around could easily judge you with. There are always these recurrent and concurrent complexes that spur *"that you"* to consciousness of what you must yield yourself for as the day starts. You can't fail yourself passing the day without fulfilling them. You are enslaved by these complexes that formed a world for you: just your world! You begin and finish a day influenced by these complexes – the way you appear in the day and clothe yourself around, and the people and things you relate with and what you do in acts and utterances will show all around you that same *'you'* who you can't do away with. You're persuaded to exercise and express your lifestyles within a concise and sufficient range of complexes. Can you imagine what is going on about you? You belong to a world you checked in with your ways.

"For where your treasure is, there will your heart be also," (Matthew 6:21).

16

You had said to yourself you got principles for running your life. Who cares, but I do! I am saying that, you are satisfied with your world may not exactly be what you must believe in. Has your world been tried with the word of God? Has it been exploited with Biblical verses? Have you forgotten you belong to God? Perhaps your choice world has provided you what you weighed to be of enough for all you care? Right! Have you considered your spiritual life? Is your spiritual self clothed with grace or naked in the world of the spirits? You are there whether you accept this or not. Your physical body shares from the spiritual world through your spiritual self even if you care not to know. The dream you just had on your bed did not include your physical body; it was just your spiritual self which was taken to see, do and finish something in your dream. It was not an imagination; it was real activity while you slept.

Don't be deceived. If your world is not unto God, it should be unto damnation. You can't take your world along to your grave when you die anyway! Yet judgement is waiting for all. Some say dreams come out of stress, but which body did you stressed if not your spiritual self that suffered mostly in all your works? Did one's body do anything without the spiritual self? All that you have done over the years have become self-structured world to contain yourself with. Howbeit, Hezekiah had said in Isaiah 38:17:

"Behold, for peace I had great bitterness; but thou hast in love to my soul delivered it from the pit of corruption: for thou hast cast all my sins behind thy back".

Take a deep breath! That skyscraper with many floors in your city harbours several activities. Its floors are many and so its height also is great. Supposing the building has no fixed elevator, what a tremendous labour one undertakes to achieve ascension and descending? To go up the floors and come down from them is very demanding and hectic. Likewise is the life of a person that is not being influenced in God's presence and which had gone astray from Christian modalities; for God had said in Isaiah 43:21:

> "...this people have I formed for myself; they shall show forth my praise".

So then, he or she lives without Christ's grace; suffering depressions and afflictions at all times. I suppose he or she is lost in a world of vanity. Then there is this offer from Jesus Christ:

> "Come unto me, all ye that labour and are heavy laden and I will give you rest", (Matthew 11:28).

Come to think of it:

> "...but the hour cometh, and now is, when the true worshippers shall worship the Father in spirit and in truth: for the Father seeketh such to worship him," (John 3:23).

And Joshua admonished:

> "Now therefore fear the LORD, and serve him in sincerity and in truth..." (Joshua 24:14).

Jeremiah let it out:

> "O LORD, the hope of Israel, all that forsake thee shall be ashamed, and they that depart from me (your Prophet) shall be written in the earth, because they have forsaken the LORD, the fountain of living waters", (Jeremiah 17:13).

Then Jesus revealed:

"For what shall it profit a man, if he shall gain the whole world, and lose his own soul? Or what shall a man give in exchange for his soul?" (Mark 8:36-37).

In conclusion, I consider the extremes to which many have yielded themselves and gone astray in projecting themselves in many things too dangerous for the spiritual self of any who must pass through eternity. No matter how great you have been in all things, and no matter how degenerated your ways have caused you, there is still hope of Salvation...

"For thus saith the Lord God, the Holy One of Israel; in returning and rest shall ye be saved; and in quietness and in confidence shall be your strength: and ye would not," (Isaiah 30:15).

Oh, why not do a rethink? Pure Christianity practices will offer strength and grace for the spiritual self of any who believes in God our Creator. Apostle Paul said:

*"Beloved, I wish above all things that thou mayest prosper and be in health, **even as thy soul prospereth,"** (3 John 1:2).*

Glory to God! Here I leave you good blessings in Jesus Name, Amen!

Chapter Two

GRACE FOR REALITIES

Realities are what every person lives to meet daily, and whether pleasant or not we need grace for them. Had you built a house as home for yourself, and an enemy says it shouldn't be you without afflictions of ill-health? Got married and unable to bear children or have a blissful stay together? Educated and but have no job? There are plans but no funds? Restlessness all nights and doctor says *'I don't know what to apply!'* Have you a family; but struggling without income for survival and say: *'I've lost sight of my true self?'*

All these are realities people experience at all times. So difficult to tell them there is God; for God's inactions, as they think, have ravaged their hearts!

Oftentimes, realities are not pleasant, but here I speak for God. To put to test God's infinite power, there is need to place before Him grim realities which when they pass away through God's visitation we say: *'for with God nothing is impossible'* or in other words *'nothing is greater than God'*.

Sometimes in one's life, he or she encounters grim realities. These realities make people cry, sorrow, and suffer some degree of depression in the midst of others; and when they overcome these ugly realities because that God intervened we must see it as **Grace for Realities**.

Honestly, unpleasant realities take away from individuals their hope and strength; and may expand to all facets of their lives. In any case, and as it has ever been, grace for realities ends their pains with wonders of God; so that people will therefore say *'there is God!'*

Life cheats on people in realities and Jesus said:

"...sufficient unto the day is the evil thereof" (Matthew 6:34).

Nevertheless, grace for realities had resolved what were more terrible than your present situations. I know that from the foundation of the world. There are Biblical proofs.

Really, no one problem can change God! Grace for Realities is His second name! He's unchangeable; and ever available to turn things around for his people. In Nigeria, people are used to the slogan, saying: *'nothing pass God!'* Hallelujah! Glory to the LORD God!

Could we easily forget the beginning of creation? The earth was without form, and void: and darkness was upon the face of the deep. And the Spirit of God moved upon the waters. And God said: *"let there be light"*, and there was light! Have you forgotten that great act and many more thereafter? If you have, then read the book of Genesis the Chapter One and you will praise the Lord God for actions and not inactions. The book of Psalms 33:4-9 says:

> *"For the word of the LORD is right; and all his works are done in truth. He loveth righteousness and judgment: the earth is full of the goodness of the LORD. By the word of the LORD were the heavens made; and all the host of them by the breath of his mouth. He gathereth the waters of the sea together as an heap: he layeth up the depth in storehouses. Let all the earth fear the LORD: let all the inhabitants of the world stand in awe of him. For he spake, and it was done; he commanded, and it stood fast".*

His creation indeed reveals wonders of grace for realities; and his doings also tell of his love for man. At one point, we should appreciate God for these people in Bible records: for they had experienced his loving kindness. Not in a little measure, because of his mercies toward man.

1. Noah's new beginning worked out:

Look at Noah after the destruction of the whole earth in the flood; overjoyed that his family had been saved. He thanked God with great collection of sacrifices that **God said in his heart**:

"I will not again curse the ground any more for man's sake... while the earth remaineth, seedtime and harvest, and cold and heat, and summer and winter, and day and night shall not cease," (Genesis 8:21-22).

Was Noah actually seeing all that which the flood had eradicated? Seedtime and harvest, and cold and heat, and summer and winter, and day and night were not things he could vision at that juncture. His joy had overridden what he needed for existence. There was life to celebrate. His family saw new dawn. Life is worth celebrating!

While Noah celebrated life, thanking God with great collection of sacrifices; grace for realities thought well for him. All things necessary for existence were set ahead of him:

"...and God blessed Noah and his sons, and said unto them, be fruitful, and multiply, and replenish the earth," (Genesis 9:1).

That's the way the LORD God is, and what he can do for anyone who will experience ugly challenges in life should not be suggested to him. He is the man's grace for unpleasant realities. Therefore be assured he will come and save you. Don't ask me when; for it could be now. Amen!

2. Sarah's barren condition ended:

Old Sarah! Did Sarah not say she was well stricken in age; and it ceased to be with her after the manner of young women to think about bearing a child? Had she not laughed within herself saying, **"After I am waxed old shall I have pleasure,**

22

my husband being old also?"

And what looks bad and impossible in the eyes of humans does not in the eye of God. His grace is sufficient for all things.

"And the LORD said unto Abraham, wherefore did Sarah laugh, saying, Shall I of a surety bear a child, which am old? **Is any thing too hard for the LORD?** *At the time appointed I will return unto thee, according to the time of life, and Sarah shall have a son,"* *(Genesis 18:13-15).*

Although Sarah denied she laughed, God looked at her and said to her "you laughed!"

Has many not done like Sarah when prophetic declarations came to them? Obviously, they have, especially when they had prayed and observed fasts and yet things remained the same.

In Sarah's case, grace for realities stood above her doubts:

"...and the LORD visited Sarah as he had said, and the LORD did unto Sarah as he had spoken. For Sarah conceived, and bare Abraham a son in his old age, at the set time of which God had spoken to him. And Abraham called the name of his son that was born unto him, whom Sarah bare to him, Isaac. And Abraham circumcised his son Isaac being eight days old, as God had commanded him...

"And Abraham was an hundred years old, when his son was born unto him. And Sarah said, God hath made me to laugh, so that all that hear will laugh with me. And she said, who would have said unto Abraham, that Sarah should have given children suck? For I have born him a son in his old age," *(Genesis 21:1-7).*

That's what he does in supply of his grace for realities.

3. Samson's one more time gave him victory:

Careless Samson! He was captured in a failed mission because of a woman; and his eyes were plucked out from him.

Fornication and lust have destroyed many like Samson was; leaving them only with a last hope. Samson was just one like some. He was chained!

Do you know many are chained too like Samson because of their errors? Some abandoned their marital relatedness because of other women or men; and some perhaps were tricked and chained with evil powers. I may not know your case, but grace for realities do. Samson exposed his hidden strength to Delillah the Philistine woman and ended up in captivity.

> *"Be sober, be vigilant, because your adversary the devil, as a roaring lion, walketh about, seeking whom he may devour; whom resist stedfast in the faith, knowing that the same afflictions are accomplished in your brethren that are in the world. **But the God of grace**, who hath called us unto his eternal glory by Christ Jesus, after that ye have suffered a while, make you perfect, stablish, strengthen, settle you," (1 Peter 5:8-10).*

Though Samson fell short of grace, it was for a while; and the LORD visited Samson and rendered him grace for realities, because he asked for it with sincere passion, saying:

> *"O LORD God, remember me, I pray thee, only this once, O God, that I may be at once avenged of the Philistines for my two eyes... and Samson said, Let me die with the Philistines..." (**Read** Judges 16:12-30).*

But would you die like Samson died with the Philistines? No! Your case does not deserve that: for you will live and declare the salvation of our God. And I should announce to you that your enemies shall die in great numbers like that of the Philistines, unless they withdraw from you in the name of Jesus! Amen!!

4. Hezekiah won fifteen more years in place of death:

Hezekiah was sick unto death. No doubt, he was going to die of it; even Prophet Isaiah had come to confirm that his time to die was decided by God Himself. Then Hezekiah prayed to God and said:

"Remember now, O LORD, I beseech thee, how I have walked before thee in truth and with a perfect heart, and have done that which is good in thy sight. And Hezekiah wept sore..." (Read Isaiah 38:1-22).

Let me ask: have you been sick and having fear that death is close? His grace for realities is bearing healing over you right now. You will be healed, and may your faith bring you healing right now in the name of Jesus Christ. Say amen and receive healing now! Amen!!

Hezekiah would die, but grace for realities erased death from him; and added fifteen more years to his days to stay alive. Let's give the Lord praise. He's faithful and merciful.

It happened! And God commanded Prophet Isaiah:

"Go, and say to Hezekiah... I have heard thy prayer, I have seen thy tears: behold, I will add unto thy days fifteen years," (Isaiah 38:5).

Wonderful grace! Hezekiah concluded that God was ready to save him, because only the living will praise the Lord. Grace for realities did it for him, and it's doing yours right now. Be healed in your body; and receive healing in your bones; your red blood and white blood cells are healed from all diseases; and right now I can see His touch on the very spot of your crises. He is the Lord. O glory to God! Hallelujah!

5. Jacob and Jabez's Status upgrade granted:

These were individuals who realized that their status should excel what they were seen to be among men. They were not sure they were enabled enough in their society. In Jacob's case, he tangled with the Lord overnight seeking a change of status when the opportunity came up. He got it! For he said to the LORD:

> *"I will not let thee go, except thou bless me. And He said unto him, what is thy name? And he said, Jacob. And He said, thy name shall be called no more Jacob, but Israel:* **for as a prince hast thou power with God and with men***, and hast prevailed," (Genesis 32:24-30).*

And Jacob acclaimed to himself: *"...I have seen God face to face, and my life is preserved." (Genesis 32:30).*

And I know you are seeing God in his loving kindness at this moment too. Your turn is now!

And Jabez's story was pathetic. Born without silver spoon, but walked with God. He followed God that he became more honourable over others in his community. Though his name indicates a child born in sorrow, he did have a God he trusted more than others. He wanted to be seen of a better status than them because he had made a difference in worship activities. Like God had said in Isaiah *43:4*:

> *"Since thou wast precious in my sight, thou hast been honourable, and I have loved thee: therefore will I give men for thee, and people for thy life."*

Did Jabez not deserve a status of honour if he had made himself precious in God's sight? Indeed his prayer to God showed he had long deserved a better status in the midst of his brethren. He prayed:

"Oh that thou wouldest bless me indeed, and enlarge my coast, and that thine hand might be with me, and that thou wouldest keep me from evil, that it may not grieve me! And God granted him that which he requested," (1 Chronicles 4:9-10).

Grace for realities was granted to Jabez and poverty and low status ended. Have you gotten the message? Nearness to God makes a person precious in his sight and honourable above others, and at all moments able to draw his grace that overcomes realities of low status in the society. You can be upgraded in the power of his might. Make a right decision from now and you will obtain his mercies. I am very sure of that. Amen!

6. Shadrach, Meshach and Abednego rescued:

They were to be roasted alive in hot fire when they failed to bow before the golden image erected by king Nebuchadnezzar. No man had dared say, *'not me to fall down and worship your pompous image,'* when a trumpet sounded.

These three resisted the king's order even if death was a punishment for that. Even at that, they held positions in the kingdom that one would not have gambled with. Then, the king in his rage and fury had commanded that they should be thrown into a burning fiery furnace for resisting worshipping his golden image. The three trusted that the God whom they served was capable of delivering them from the hot fire. What a faith?

"...And He will deliver us out of thine hand, O king, but if not, be it known unto thee, O king, that we will not serve thy gods, nor worship the golden image which thou hast set up," **(Read Daniel 3:1-30)**.

God declared in **Isaiah 43:1-2**, saying:

"...fear not, for I have redeemed thee, I have called

thee by thy name: thou art mine... when thou walkest through the fire, thou shalt not be burned; neither shall the flame kindle upon thee."

It was so, that the mighty men that took up Shadrach, Meshach, and Abednego were slew of the flame of the fire, because it was exceeding hot to escape from. Grace for realities was readily available for the three; they were unhurt, and the king's eyes were opened to see the mighty hand of God saving the condemned. Astounded, he rose up in haste, and said to his counsellors:

"Did not we cast three men bound into the midst of the fire? Lo, I see four men loose, walking in the midst of the fire, and they have no hurt; and the form of the fourth is like the Son of God," (Daniel 4:24).

Hallelujah! Awesome! Had he said it, and would he not do it? Give glory to God!

7. David's economic victory proclaimed:

Grace for grim realities were proclaimed by David; and seeing the world of men that by strength shall no man prevail, he subdued his fear of economy distress, saying in **Psalm 23:1-6**:

"The LORD is my shepherd; I shall not want. He maketh me to lie down in green pastures: he leadeth me beside the still waters. He restoreth my soul: he leadeth me in the paths of righteousness for his name's sake...

"Yea, though I walk through the valley of the shadow of death, I will fear no evil: for thou art with me; thy rod and thy staff they comfort me. Thou preparest a table before me in the presence of mine enemies: thou anointest my head with oil; my cup runneth over.

Surely goodness and mercy shall follow me all the days of my life: and I will dwell in the house of the LORD for ever," **Amen!**

David's view of economy distress proved that God's grace for realities which all believers must live with in times of hardship are achievable. Whatever may be one's experience in the days of economic hardship is not weighed above His grace. He or she still exists under the Lord's grace. With God nothing is impossible. Possessing possessions is possible; experiencing good health is possible; and comfort is possible! His eye is upon them that hope in his mercy; to deliver their soul from death, and to keep them alive in famine. (Read Psalms 33:18-22).

Isaac was stopped from leaving his place of abode to Egypt for reason of famine, and the LORD blessed him in the days of famine. (Read Genesis 26:1-25).

Looking into all these wonders, let us agree that our God makes things possible in cases of all impossibilities. Let's bless him ahead of our own wonders and miracles in times of grim realities.

8. The awesomeness of the Lord unfolded:

The book of **Proverbs 30:21-23** reveals thus:

"For three things the earth is disquieted, and for four which it cannot bear: for a servant when he reigneth; and a fool when he is filled with meat; for an odious woman when she is married; and an handmaid that is heir to her mistress."

Have you taken your own deep breath? I have! What should be more overwhelming? An odious woman will not be rejected because of grace of possibility. A maidservant will rule over her mistress' inheritance. A servant will reign when God says so. May you not be a fool; but even if you have been, transformation will happen.

29

I said it; God is awesome! Do you see all these? Oh! It's happening already! A single lady will be joined too soon with a young flourishing gentle man; don't say *'impossible!'* because it can happen! Watch out for a miracle!!!

When Mary said to the Angel: *"how shall this be? The Angel answered her: For with God nothing shall be impossible. Then, Mary said: Lord; be it unto me according to thy word,"* **(Read Luke 1:26-38)**.

Rejoice O people of God for the Lord's grace upon us: for he shall supply all our needs according to his riches in glory. His word says in **Psalm 37:1-7**:

> *"Fret not thyself because of evildoers, neither be thou envious against the workers of iniquity. For they shall soon be cut down like the grass, and wither as the green herb. Trust in the LORD, and do good; so shalt thou dwell in the land, and verily thou shalt be fed. Delight thyself also in the LORD: and he shall give thee the desires of thine heart...*

> *"Commit thy way unto the LORD; trust also in him; and he shall bring it to pass. And he shall bring forth thy righteousness as the light, and thy judgment as the noonday. Rest in the LORD, and wait patiently for him: fret not thyself because of him who prospereth in his way, because of the man who bringeth wicked devices to pass."*

His grace will sort out all things for man when there is trust. Let's hallow his name once again! Blessing today!

Chapter Three

HIDDEN STRENGTH

Hidden strength in view is the *'intuitive alertness'* inherent in humans which is immensely able to enforce, influence, and judge all things whatsoever; but not yet discovered and induced by many because of ignorance. Man was created firstly to apply *intuitive alertness* which makes up his *spiritual nature* without the use of the mind, (Read Genesis 2:25; 3:6-7).

Take a deep breath! Looking at yourself it is not the mind that tells you that you are a male or female, and also not the mind that tells you that you are alive; but the mind is only present when you are for instead misaddressed as a male or female and in the case of your wellbeing when your existence is threatened by ailments. That spontaneous power to know that you are a male or female and that you're alive without applying your mind is what *intuitive alertness* is; and it's inherent in all humans and also covers all areas of their lives except in areas of cares for selves where conscious reasoning is applied.

Human nature is based on two-way alertness which the heart suffers to manage momentarily – the *intuitive alertness* which transports spiritual realities to the heart; and the *mind alertness* which also transports life issues and desires to the heart of a human being: but the intuitive alertness and the mind alertness will ever function contrarily unless a person is sober, (1Peter 5:8-9). **Take note: that the senses of man are what the entire mind alertness offers.**

Humans are ultimately spiritual entity in their image and likeness of God, but a great number of people are quite very ignorant of their hidden strength because of the closeness of life issues and desires to them than their spiritual nature.

However, the alertness from one's mind coming to the heart momentarily might be higher than the spontaneous alertness done by power of intuition simply because such person is not yet spiritual. In this the word of God means a lot to our souls.

That baby just being delivered by a mother is crying not with the mind alertness but with intuitive alertness demanding for things he or she could not just think about how to get them. That baby is verily spiritual at that stage without knowledge of physical desires which the mind alertness offers – the mind is yet not active. When being mishandled we say *'he's a baby!'*

> *"And Jesus called a little child unto him, and set him in the midst of them. And said, Verily I say unto you, except ye be converted, and become as little children, ye shall not enter into the kingdom of heaven. Whosoever therefore shall humble himself as this little child, the same is greatest in the kingdom of heaven,"* *(Matthew 18:2-4).*

As the baby grows to adulthood, the intuitive power is being suppressed gradually because of self-inclined behaviour besides closeness of life issues and desires created by mind alertness: and if not redirected by the word of God, he or she becomes a prey to the devils which is no more going to be good for him or her. This is exactly the way it is with all except the word of God is allowed to enter therein. Your heaven won't come!

> *"Thy word is a lamp unto my feet, and a light unto my path,"* *(Psalm 119:105).*

Jeremiah was told of his hidden strength when the LORD God visited him to open up to him his unknown strength inherent in him, saying:

> *"Before I formed thee in the belly I know thee: and before thou camest forth out of the womb I sanctify*

thee, and I ordained thee a prophet unto the nations..."
(Read Jeremiah 1:5-10).

Jesus Christ our Lord had spoken and transmitted strength to his disciples on many occasions, in facts; variety of impartations capable of awakening those who will find wisdom therefrom. Hear him:

"For I will give you a mouth and wisdom, which all your adversaries shall not be able to gainsay nor resist," (Luke 21:15).

"And when he had called unto him his disciples, he gave them power against unclean spirits, to cast them out, and to heal all manner of sickness and all manner of disease," (Matthew 10:1).

"Verily I say unto you, Whatsoever ye shall bind on earth shall be bound in heaven; and whatsoever ye shall loose on earth shall be loosed in heaven," (Matthew 18:18).

"And these signs shall follow them that believe; In my name shall they cast out devils; they shall speak with new tongues; They shall take up serpents; and if they drink any deadly thing, it shall not hurt them; they shall lay hands on the sick, and they shall recover," (Mark 16:17-18).

These all tell of transmitted and also bequeathed strength to believers: we are endowed with them and are yet to be induced by some believers; or rather they have no ideas how invisible things could be enforced, influenced and judged to manifest physically by them. If they achieved all these by ***intuitive alertness***, we say they exercised faith in God and performed

33

miracles.

(*Faith takes what does not actually present itself physically from where it is hidden in the spiritual world, or demands for it to manifest, either by enforcing, influencing, and judging to make room for it to manifest*).

Our Lord Jesus once said to his disciples of their ignorance of the manner of spirit they were made of when James and John required of him to permit them to command fire to come down from heaven to consume certain villagers just as Elijah did because they saw them despised their Master Jesus Christ. He rebuked them, saying: *"ye know not what manner of spirit ye are of,"* *(Luke 9:51).* They could have achieved that in faith induced by intuitiveness.

Let's look back again to the beginning when Adam and Eve were naked and they were not ashamed, (Genesis 2:25). That was their intuitive experience and the relatedness between them and God was by intuition. And they were deceived by the serpent and ate of the fruit of knowledge of good and evil and their eyes were opened: in other explanation the mind was enabled by the fruit to provoke conscious reasoning of good and evil through the sense organs, (Genesis 3:6-7).

And they were no more relying on intuitive nature only as they were firstly created to be. Life issues and desires and self-inclined choices were closer to their hearts because of mind alertness than intuitive reality that quickens spiritual nature; and the lust of the eyes, and the lust of the flesh, and the pride of life became their death which God had warned them about. They both were growing spiritually dead, because their power of intuition was gradually being suppressed in the face of closeness of life issues and desires generated by mind alertness.

The intake of the good and evil fruit gave them knowledge of choices and desires as their minds came alive. They lived with that in self-defence and self-righteousness. At that point, they started losing their intuitive powers to lust which the mind offered them, even in accusing each other before God. Their hearts were unstable and lustfully inclined to self-righteousness more than of the intuitive nature they had been and were sinless.

34

Remember, when our Lord Jesus was asked which is the first commandment of all by one of the scribes, he instructed him to love the LORD God with all his **heart, soul, mind,** and **strength**, (Read Mark 12:28-32). These parts of human are character enforcing. These character enforcers are in humans to suppress intuitive powers in them if not checked. When you neglect intuitive alertness to these character enforcers it is clear you have lost your spirituality. Your heart becomes deceitful and craving for self-indulgences which are seen as self-righteousness. Therefore Jesus had said:

"...take no thought, saying, What shall we eat? or, What shall we drink? or, Wherewithal shall we be clothed?" (Matthew 6:31).

He was engaged to save people from destroying their spiritual alertness enjoyed through intuition. Life issues and desires suppress our spiritual state if the heart, soul, mind, and strength which are character enforcers are not redirected to loving God first. And He further said that man shall not live by bread alone but by every word that proceeds from the mouth of God, (Matthew 4:4). Bread for flesh and his word for man's soul! God was actually interested in the manifestation of his own – they that look unto his Son's wisdom, (John 3:16). And living in the spirit will ever be of a bettered life than we know it. Therefore *intuitive alertness* should be tied to faith.

"Behold, his soul which is lifted up is not upright in him: but the just shall live by faith," (Habakkuk 2:4).

Very obvious the soul men lift up to God is not upright in them because of self-inclined choices besides closeness of life issues and desires: but live in absence of intuitions which had shattered trust in God, and those who will receive from heaven must live by faith. Faith works better with intuitive alertness than the mind alertness. Let me define faith more easily for you. Faith

35

is: *just spontaneously knowing that there is God to believe on, and all what he is able to do, and must worship him for manifestations, and act according to his word.*

Yeah! You got faith right! This will automatically create in you the substance of things you directed your hope on; and also the evidence of those things manifesting even if you have not seen them, (Hebrews 11:1, 6).

Faith helps in fetching from the spiritual world all things enabled by God. Do you need divine interventions? Do you wish to manifest the life of God? Faith will connect you! But your faith will need your intuitiveness if it must draw results. You must have the need to stir up your intuitive powers which are inherent in you to make faith to work.

Emotionally still mind is intuitiveness prompting when we are in spiritual business. A still mind prevents doubts and enables one's intuitive powers to come alive for faith to work. Intuition will come alive with all that God is in **power, wisdom, blessing, riches, glory, might, and honour**: for they are embedded in our living soul in order to link humans to his grace, (Romans 1:19). And do not give the mind a chance to weigh matters for you if you must achieve results, (Read 2Corinthians 10:3-5). Apostle Paul pushed this harder, saying:

> *"Now the just shall live by faith: but if any man draw back, my soul shall have no pleasure in him. But we are not of them who draw back unto perdition; but of them that believe to the saving of the soul," (Hebrews 10:38-39)*

Perfect counsel! A child of perdition is one that has lost totally the power of intuition which helps understand God and his works better. Then do not say you have faith in God when you have lost intuitive powers! The hidden strength has fainted in many. Some don't even know it. And the Lord said:

"if ye had faith as a grain of mustard seed, ye might say unto this sycamine tree, Be thou plucked up by the root, and be thou planted in the sea; and should obey you," (Luke 17:6).

If that be the case, you and I can do great works, if we work out our salvation intuitively thus:

1. Hidden Strength of Power:

To operate in power one has to battle away imaginable formations stored in the core of his or her heart concerning other powers that exist on earth where humans dwell; but giving room for rousing intuitions of what the Almighty whom one believes on is in power. Do not consider anything too high above what knowledge you have of God in power play, drawing in such grace God shed over those he had supported in times of power interface. Engender a still mind so that the rising intuition will fill your heart with divine information.

As much as in you, let your heart be filled with conquering spirits and let your thoughts that allow fears be suppressed in readiness to overcome all illicit and evil spells poised before you. Be willing to dismiss any charging idea rising from your mind to make you have doubts. Count on your enforcing spirits created by intuition at the moments of impending warfare and never lose them by working of the mind. Heroic influences will be revealed in you by a sudden searching intuition machine at work. Depend on such revelations and enforce them independent of the state of the heart, and beholding the Almighty God whom you serve in this, you will enter a realm of power; and might begin to utter words of power before you know it, (Read 2Corinthians 10:3-5).

In the days of King Saul's reign when Goliath subjected the people of God to trembling, young David said to Saul: ***"let no man's heart fail because of him; thy servant will go and fight with this Philistine."*** And he did not allow the fears of the mind have effects on him. He moved forward to conquer a giant

Goliath, saying, *"The LORD that delivered me out of the paw of the lion, and out of the paw of the bear, he will deliver me out of the hand of this Philistine."* His intuitive powers prevailed in directing him on what he must observe to do, and then said to Goliath: *"thou comest to me with a sword, and with a spear, and with a shield: but I come to thee in the name of the LORD of hosts, the God of the armies of Israel, who thou hast defiled."*

Read the whole book of (**1 Samuel 17**) and view what intuitive powers achieved for young David. The strong in the spiritual world are those who draw strength from intuitions: **for what intuition offers come from the living soul** which men call inspiration. Elijah cut down the prophets of Baal, and Samson avenged his eyes upon the Philistines, (Read 1Kings 18 and Judges 16).

You too! You will conquer the enemy in Jesus Name, amen! Your sleepless nights will end, and shrines from where you are troubled will be razed, and the wicked and the devils will have dread of you, in the name of Jesus! Amen!

Constant yielding to intuitions stirs up inner power that allows a stable heart especially in trouble periods; the mind may not be helpful in times of tribulations.

2. Hidden Strength of Wisdom:

"Wisdom is the principal thing, therefore get wisdom: and with all thy getting get understanding. Exalt her, and she shall promote thee: she shall bring thee to honour, when thou embrace her," (Proverbs 4:7-8).

Wisdom helps to see things the way they are, and sometimes misconstrued as intelligence. Intelligence is achieved by the alertness of the mind, while wisdom is acquired by intuitive alertness. Bring both together, humans beget wonderful accomplishments.

The conflict of wisdom and intelligence has confused many, and people like to claim both as what made them what they are. But not exactly so: for wisdom excels above intelligence:

38

because understanding will defect intellectual protocols and make wisdom true of what it offers. Because wisdom springs forth by intuitive alertness, it goes in search of an unction which also will be intuitively provided to make all things have their right placements. That's what understanding is!

> *"But ye have an unction from the Holy One, and ye know all things," (1John 2:20).*

> *"Howbeit when he, the Spirit of truth, is come, he will guide you into all truth: for he shall not speak of himself; but whatsoever he shall hear, that shall he speak: and he will shew you things to come," (John 16:13).*

Now, when one's intuition springs forth with knowledge of wisdom, I advise that one should not immediately work with all that he or she found in wisdom; but to get understanding which helps in making wisdom different from intellectual influences. Understanding is very scarce when the mind is at work. Therefore excuse your mind to get understanding through same intuitive alertness. The spirit of understanding requires stillness of the mind so that your spiritual self (the soul) can intuitively know how to apply what wisdom offered. King Solomon was indeed intuitive when two harlots fought over a living child while the other was dead, (Read 1Kings 3:16-28). For the King to demand for a sword to divide the living baby into two is wisdom gotten by intuition. And when one of the harlots pressed to see the baby died, understanding aroused in the King's heart that no true mother will want her baby dead! The true mother of the child enjoyed divine intervention.

> *"Then the king answered and said, Give her the living child, and in no wise slay it: she is the mother thereof. And all Israel heard of the judgment which the king had judged; and they feared the king; for they saw that*

the wisdom of God was in him, to do judgment,"
(1Kings 3:27-28).

*"If the ax is dull, and one does not sharpen the edge,
then he must use more strength, but wisdom brings
success," (Ecclesiastes 10:10 NKJV).* **Or "...wisdom is
profitable to direct," (KJV).**

*"Get wisdom; get understanding: forget it not; neither
decline from the words of my mouth. Forsake her not,
and she shall preserve thee: love her, and she shall
keep thee," (Proverbs 4:5-6).*

*"Who is as the wise man? and who knoweth the
interpretation of a thing? a man's wisdom maketh his
face to shine, and the boldness of his face shall be
changed," (Ecclesiastes 8:1).*

The key words are that; the mind attains to intelligence
while intuition arouses to wisdom and draw understanding thereto
to cause success in one's life. Therefore, develop your heart to
work with intuitiveness more than what the mind alertness offers.
Then Satan can ever be defeated just as it was when Jesus spent
forty days in the wilderness in fasts. (Read Matthew 4:1-11;
Proverbs 8:1-36).

If you must be spiritual, use the mind only when
structuring and composing what makes life's positiveness and
worth living; but live out your life (most part of the day) induced
by intuitions. Wisdom and understanding come by intuitiveness;
for it's the domain of God's entrance into one's life.

3. Hidden Strength of Blessing:

"The blessing of the LORD, it maketh rich, and **he
addeth no sorrow with it**,*" (Proverbs 10:22).*

Whatever level of breakthrough one enjoys along with pains of life is without the preserving power of spiritual living. In other words, such blessing came forth either both partly godly and ungodly, or totally ungodly: for God will not, and here I repeat this: God will not add sorrow to his blessings for his people. The enemy may be seen in certain times of suffering along with blessing as a plague to what we earned in life. Such plague would happen because certain ordinances of the LORD God were handled with hesitancy or even despised.

Alright! How does one's mind-set bring evil around him where blessings are visible? And where does intuition save one's blessing?

Judging from all angles, no one life experiences a day of existence without spiritual input: and at the same time, no one life is expected to pass through a day without spiritual output. Everyone a living is indebted to the *world of life* which in it all natures are sustained; even for the air consumed and other gifts of nature we are enjoying on daily basis. These are spiritual input that deserves humans' spiritual output to the Provider, the God of the earth. And yet humans cheat on God.

Whether you like to know this or not, cheating has been one seat for inverted evils. Cheating covers all acts being deceptive, fraudulent, unfaithful, dishonest, disloyal, etc. And cheating paves way for evils to sail along with one's blessings. Cheating is common to humans because the mind always seek for self first in all things that have tangibility and behavioural composition. The humans always want to support themselves first with anything they desired and that are seen sufficient for their needs: and selflessness is very rare in the heart of a human being. In doing this, they end up disobeying God and subverting sacred demands to their detriment. They cheat one another and care not; and they had robbed divinity and looked away. But God had spoken:

"Even from the days of your fathers ye are gone away from mine ordinances, and have not kept them. Return

unto me, and I will return unto you, saith the LORD of hosts. But ye said, Wherein shall we return? Will a man rob God? Yet ye have robbed me. But ye say, Wherein have we robbed thee? In tithes and offerings. Ye are cursed with a curse: for ye have robbed me, even this whole nation," (Malachi 3:7-9).

This is one part of cheating that can expose other ways of it among humans. They steal, subdue, covet, manipulate, trick, and do whatever comes forth to enrich themselves with; and definitely will still deny God his portion – penitence, obedience, and fellowship. Don't forget this, that divine blessing encompasses all what allow peace of one's life and also brings joy to a person round the clock. If peace and joy are broken away in the middle of what he or she claims to be blessing there is need to examine self in areas of cheating generated by mind alertness. Satan comes, and Satan does not engender much of evil in godly blessing, except he has to collect what you retained by cheating man and God! Such cheatings were so many that you can't remember them all.

"When thou vowest a vow unto God, defer not to pay it; for he hath no pleasure in fools: pay that which thou hast vowed. Better is it that thou shouldest not vow, than that thou shouldest vow and not pay. Suffer not thy mouth to cause thy flesh to sin; neither say thou before the angel, that it was an error: wherefore should God be angry at thy voice, and destroy the work of thine hands?" (Ecclesiastes 5:4-6).

"Withhold not good from them to whom it is due, when it is in the power of thine hand to do it. Say not unto thy neighbour, Go, and come again, and tomorrow I will give; when thou hast it by thee. Devise not evil against thy neighbour, seeing he dwelleth securely by thee..." (Read Proverbs 3:27-35).

But yielding to intuitiveness had sustained the blessings of those whose hearts were instigated to perform all what they envisaged by intuitions. You must have heard someone said: *'something moved me to do, or prompted this act, and thereafter I received these miracles.'*

Intuitions provide divine feelings. And when you attained to divine consciousness, your blessing stays without sorrow. Remember Job was a man given to Satan by God himself to destroy all that he had and yet did not depart from righteousness until a restoration was again experienced. Hear job:

*"Though he slay me, yet will I trust in him: but **I will maintain mine own ways before him**," (Job 13:15).*

Thank God for Job. That was an intuitive self-admonition. Believe on intuitions and be inspired thereof to perform godly ordinances as provided by the word of God and you shall be comforted with godly blessings, (Matthew 5:6). And you're spiritual already!

4. Hidden Strength of Riches:

There can't be anything like riches; for riches show what money can provide, and money provides answer for all things, (Ecclesiastes 10:19). And Apostle Paul had said:

"Beloved, I wish above all things that thou mayest prosper and be in health, even as thy soul prospereth," (3 John 1:2).

Wealth is a gift for individuals from God, particularly his people; but not without tactful commitments which ensure distribution and outreach efforts to attend to others' needs, and even God's folks. Moses had admonished the Israelites, saying:

"Lest when thou hast eaten and art full, and hast built goodly houses, and dwelt therein; and when thy herds

43

*and thy flocks multiply, and thy silver and thy gold is multiplied, and all that thou hast is multiplied; then thine heart be lifted up, and thou forget the LORD thy God, which brought thee forth out of the land of Egypt, from the house of bondage... and thou say in thine heart, My power and the might of mine hand hath gotten me this wealth. But thou shalt remember the LORD thy God: for it is he that giveth thee power to get wealth, that **he may establish his covenant** which he sware unto thy fathers, as it is this day,"* (Deuteronomy 8:12-18).*

This was quite a pronounced alertness that a loyal believer must be adapting to doing while heaven provides for him or her abundantly. Be relevant to the source of your riches. Even Apostle Paul wasn't really sure of compliance and for this reason he ended up wishing that one may prosper and be in health even as his or her soul prospers. Yeah! The soul firstly must be influenced, and enforced to comply with all that pave ways for riches. Have you thought about something like these verses?

"Bring ye all the tithes into the storehouse, that there may be meat in mine house, and prove me now herewith, saith the LORD of hosts, if I will not open you the windows of heaven, and pour you out a blessing, that there shall not be room enough to receive it. And I will rebuke the devourer for your sakes, and he shall not destroy the fruits of your ground; neither shall your vine cast her fruit before the time in the field, saith the LORD of hosts," (Malachi 3:10-11).

Do not end up in the hands of devouring powers before you get wise on this clarion call. Even Jesus Christ added his voice, saying:

"Give, and it shall be given unto you, good measure, pressed down, and shaken together, and running over,

shall men give into your bosom. For with the same measure that ye mete withal it shall be measured to you again," (Luke 6:38).

Apostle Paul came up with what looks better in driving home how one can be blessed with riches, and he said:

*"I have shewed you all things, how that so labouring ye ought to support the weak, and to remember the words of the Lord Jesus, how he said, **It is more blessed to give than to receive,"** (Acts 20:35).*

"But this I say, He which soweth sparingly shall reap also sparingly; and he which soweth bountifully shall reap also bountifully. Every man according as he purposeth in his heart, so let him give; not grudgingly, or of necessity: for God loveth a cheerful giver. And God is able to make all grace abound toward you; that ye, always having all sufficiency in all things, may abound to every good work: (As it is written, He hath dispersed abroad; he hath given to the poor: his righteousness remaineth for ever," 2 Corinthians 9:6-9).

When one's attitude of giving is based on possibility and done grudgingly, or waiting for a third party to bring to his or her notice to do the needful, such persons will never experience heavenly sources of wealth and riches.

"Therefore say I unto you, The kingdom of God shall be taken from you, and given to a nation bringing forth the fruits thereof," (Matthew 21:43).

On this I say, riches come not by hoping on one's wishes but by practical sowing and reaping according to his word. Prayers to get riches are good when one has developed an attitude of sowing bountifully from the little he had gotten (Mark 12:41-44). Let not your mind conflict deceives you, but let your heart be intuitively influenced and enforced to judge well all things. If your heart rest upon its mind alertness you will be the first to suffer its wickedness.

> *"The heart is deceitful above all things, and desperately wicked: who can know it," (Jeremiah 17:9).*

And you will be able to control your self-wilfulness when you are intuitively inclined concerning all matters.

5. Hidden Strength of Glory:

> *"Arise, shine; for thy light is come, and the glory of the LORD is risen upon thee," (Isaiah 60:1).*

Glories are solely possessed by God, and in his magnanimous love he does portray his glory in mankind. When men talk about their own glories, they are limited to what are perishable, and make no mistake; human glories are like the grass that withers.

> *"For all flesh is as grass, and all the glory of man as the flower of grass. The grass withereth, and the flower thereof falleth away," (1Peter 1:24).*

Glory is what is overwhelming and powerful in nature having a phenomenon well adored by watchers, and capable of being related to many wonders that have their bearings on humans. God's own glories are not equitable; for he will never share his glory with any man; in power and appearance, though certain people are raised to show forth his praise, (Isaiah 43:21). These set of people are not underestimated in demonstration of the abilities of the Almighty.

"Elijah was a man with a nature like ours, and he prayed earnestly that it would not rain; and it did not rain on the land for three years and six months. And he prayed again, and the heaven gave rain, and the earth produced its fruit," (James 5:17-18 NKJV).

If you cannot consider what you can do in life to bring you up in the eyes of men, an offer had been made; saying, *'arise, shine...'* for when it matters. These two words cannot be envisioned unless you are intuitive in nature. There are going to be proactive steps, and efforts, and tendencies drawn from intuitive revelations about the awesomeness of the Almighty God in performances. Because of what Moses had seen of the Almighty God, he had said to Pharaoh:

"...Glory over me: when shall I intreat for thee, and for thy servants, and for thy people, to destroy the frogs from thee and thy houses, that they may remain in the river only," (Exodus 8:9).

Showing forth the Lord's praise is proving his glories to men on earth. The extraordinary miracles and the surprises seen of great manifestation of wonders by those who were moved intuitively to prove God's worth to men are the glories demonstrated by them based on what they foreknew of God. The likes of Moses, Joshua, Elijah, Peter and others who performed wonders in their times were not moved by mind alertness: for the mind will waver in time of critical issues.

To demonstrate the Lord's glory is to start actions that create a cloud of his glory over man, but you don't do them because you are lost in a world of mental tendencies, and where humans depart not from inappropriate passions. Inappropriate passion is darkness over people caused by mind alertness which make them forget what God is in glory. But keep these abreast!

"All things were made by him; and without him was not any thing made that was made. In him was life; and

47

the life was the light of men. And the light shineth in darkness; and the darkness comprehended it not," (John 1:3-5)

"For in him we live, and move, and have our being..." (Acts 17:28).

"Jesus answered them, Is it not written in your law, I said, Ye are gods? If he called them gods, unto whom the word of God came, and the scripture cannot be broken..." (Read John 10:34-38).

I know, you're not left out! And I know, you can shine forth in demonstration of his glory. Begin to see the fullness of him in you as you start the day.

"For, behold, the darkness shall cover the earth, and gross darkness the people but the LORD shall arise upon thee, and his glory shall be seen upon thee," (Isaiah 60:2).

6. Hidden Strength of Might:

One's spiritual might indicates his ability to command things to be or behave, in the order he chooses them to be or behave, irrespective of what they were before they were affected by such command. Jesus was on a journey back to the city one morning and was hungry and desired to eat something. Seeing a fig tree blossom with leaves, he approached it to eat of its fruit; and was disappointed to find nothing from it to eat, and he said to it with intent of ending his fruitfulness, saying: *"...let no fruit grow on thee henceforward for ever,"* and immediately the fig tree withered. And when the disciples saw it, they marvelled, saying, how soon the fig tree is withered away! (Read Matthew 21:18-20).

In the day when the LORD delivered up the Amorites

before the children of Israel, Joshua commanded the Sun and the Moon to reposition themselves over their enemies in order to accomplish fully their victory.

"And the sun stood still, and the moon stayed, until the people had avenged themselves upon their enemies..." (Joshua 10:11-13).

These are acts God wants his children on earth to achieve as evidence of his presence in them. Jeremiah had said:

"...the LORD put forth his hand, and touched my mouth. And the LORD said unto me, Behold, I have put my words in thy mouth. See, I have this day set thee over the nations and over the kingdoms, to root out, and to pull down, and to destroy, and to throw down, to build, and to plant," (Jeremiah 1:9-10).

And the LORD had encouraged Jeremiah of his readiness to perform all the acts thereof. Had God not said to Zerubbabel, saying: **"not by might, nor by power, but by my spirit?"** which makes the fact that intuitiveness (*which is God's connection with the soul of man by his spirit*) can only influence mighty deeds. Jesus said these signs shall follow us who believe. (Read Zechariah 4:6; Mark 16:17-18). Our Lord Jesus also had answered his disciples after the fig tree episode, saying to them:

"Verily I say unto you, if ye have faith, and doubt not, ye shall not only do this which is done to the fig tree, but also if ye shall say unto this mountain, Be thou removed, and be thou cast into the sea; it shall be done. And all things, whatsoever ye shall ask in prayer, believing, ye shall receive," (Matthew 21:21-22).

Now these verses brings me back to what I earlier indicated regarding the workability of faith... *to stir up your intuitive powers which are inherent in you to make faith to work: for your faith will need your hidden strength if it must draw results. A still mind prevents doubts and enables one's intuitive powers to come alive for faith to work.* Therefore, move in the power of his might.

7. Hidden Strength of Honour:

Honour in this sense is having spiritual value which reflects what one has spiritually attained above others. Honour draws recognition of others when it gets God's approval. Sometimes honourable positions are bought by affluence and well-doing in the midst of others who have taken much from such individuals. These kinds are thrusts on others whether be they genuine or not. But in this text I should talk about honour ordained by the LORD God based on one's relationship with him.

Enoch was someone seen in the Bible as somebody who walked with God: and he was not tracked; for God took him away, (Genesis 5:22-24). Noah's case among the first societies of humankind was a situation of Noah labouring for a hundred years to attend to God's plan to end the first world; and he found favour in the sight of God because of unrelenting fellowship with God, (Read Genesis chapters **7** and **8**). Elijah lived all his life following God's interests without a record of a descendant. A great numbers of individuals attained to honourable relationship with God that even God himself said of Abraham:

> *"...shall I hide from Abraham that thing which I do; seeing that Abraham shall surely become a great and mighty nation, and all the nations of the earth shall be blessed in him? For I know him, that he will command his children and his household after him, and they shall keep the way of the LORD, to do justice and judgment; that the LORD may bring upon Abraham that which he hath spoken of him," (Genesis 18:17-19)*

And Abraham retained an honour throughout generations that is still being upheld until date. His honour was linked to all

50

his descendants through Isaac and Jacob. Should we forget easily how he could have offered his only old age son, Isaac, for God's sake? We know others in the Bible that are exemplars unto this day. They gave us a reason to follow our Creator! (Read Romans 4:1-16; Hebrews 11:1-16).

But Peter almost lost his honour and our Lord Jesus promptly reached him, demanding of his love for him: when Peter subjected his heart to what senses offer; reminding him to feed His sheep, (John 21:15-17). And there are divine gains in unrelenting fellowship with the Lord. When God had considered Israel as in Jacob, he then said to him:

"...fear not: for I have redeemed thee, I have called thee by thy name; thou art mine. When thou passest through the waters, I will be with thee; and through the rivers, they shall not overflow thee: when thou walkest through the fire, thou shalt not be burned; neither shall the flame kindle upon thee... **Since thou wast precious in my sight, thou hast been honourable,** *and I have loved thee; therefore will I give men for thee, and people for thy life..." (Read Isaiah 43).*

That Jabez was more honourable than his brethren was wrongly interpreted by many preachers as being his poverty condition, (1Chronicles 4:9-10). Would one so become precious in God's sight because he was poor in his time? I will doubt that. And I will disagree as well. God cannot be mutilated to recognize who is not relatively knotted to him in fellowship, whether be poor or not, to gain approval of self honourable desires when he or she asks for them like Jabez did. On this I speak for the LORD God. To be honourable in the sight of God to gain recognition as highlighted in the above verses is but one's unrelenting relationship with God.

The big question now is; can anyone with unstable mind alertness achieve approval of his honour tag?

"But he that glorieth, let him glory in the Lord. For not he that commendeth himself is approved, but whom the Lord commendeth," (2 Corinthians 10:17-18).

Remember this always: intuition power is inherent in humans and our spirituality must be sourced from the soul from where it's stored; for it's the domain of God's entrance into one's life. Blessing today! And may his Grace be unto you!

Chapter Four

CONSEQUENCES OF UNBELIEF

Unbelief is a functioning weakness found in a person who will not accept within comprehension what he or she doubted, or has not personally experienced, even if he or she had witnessed people who experienced theirs; and in most cases, things that are invisible and incorporeal. Unbelief is a lifestyle.

Unfortunately, unbelieving lifestyles exist in people who consider only what are physically handled as things that are sure. Pardon me to say they are short-sighted in knowing and seeing things that have eluded their comprehensibility; and they allow themselves to be subdued by their depressive reasoning which terminates all things that are not acceptable to them from their hearts, even if they result in arguments.

Unbelief is a basement for the devils, giving no chance for recovery especially when the person in question will not open up for spiritual influences that can save him or her.

"When the unclean spirit is gone out of a man, he walketh through dry places, seeking rest, and findeth none. Then he saith, I will return into my house from whence I came out, and when he is come, he findeth it empty, swept, and garnished. Then goeth he, and taketh with himself seven other spirits more wicked than himself, and they enter in and dwell there: and the last state of that man is worse than the first. Even so shall it be also unto this wicked generation," (Matthew 12:43-45).

The man spoken of had indeed received divine liberation from an evil spirit's possession, and unbelief disposition blinded him from seeing the reality of salvation which he had experienced. His enemy checked back, and seeing his earlier host was in ignorance of divine intervention through unbelieving lifestyles, the unclean spirit returned with seven more wicked spirits to make his latter state of mind worse than the former. And in like manner was the world of men weighed by the Lord.

Even then, he had grown habits from his former self whom he did not fight to drop because of unbelief toward what were unseen and unphysical: though he tangibly felt some signs of emptiness and lightness elation in moments of times, yet his transformation for the time being he had not trusted to be necessary encounters. All of that, as he thought, were hallucinations; if not of it a delusion depriving him of certainty of his former self which he knew better; and willingness to continue his self-styled life was compelling and enticing. Then he lost a chance to be saved to his enemy.

The unclean spirit knew how weakly unbelief had rendered his host's spiritual self, and he returned this time more fortified. To break into such life with gospeling truth might draw rebellion.

Unbelieving lifestyles block divine influences and providential gains which come from God: for indeed there is no unbelief except that man and God must relate. God's connection to man is spiritually designed whether you want to accept it or not. Man enjoys physicality, while God manages invisibleness. And the incompatibility that exists between God and man is the unbelief that humans develop over times.

> *But the natural man receiveth not the things of the Spirit of God: for they are foolishness unto him: neither can he know them, because they are spiritually discerned, (1 Corinthians 2:14).*

Considering the above verse places a person in the natural characteristics, we see him or her broken off from the supernatural charisma which can place him or her above self-imposed lifestyles. Supernaturalism opens up a person to divinity, and this is the best form he or she should be reactive to so that he or she could examine all things as God allows them. The person authorizes his or her lifestyles in the prompting of the Holy Spirit, and not being judged by any in all spiritual doings.

"But he that is spiritual judgeth all things, yet he himself is judged of no man," (1 Corinthians 2:15).

Unbelief disconnects you from seeing God's world properly. And you exist in his creation until death calls you out. But what would you change in a world you cannot envisage the powers that rule it? The world of men is in the control of powers which are beyond the mentalities of humans that occupy it. But God is known as the Supreme over them all, (1 Samuel 2:3-8).

This you must know: that all the powers that rule the world of men are spiritually designed; even for humans to be able to exist together and regard one another is spiritually influenced. To share in love is spiritually influenced; and to war among humans is as well spiritually influenced. The behaviours of humans are spiritually manoeuvred. And to prosper and be in health are spiritually influenced, even to live long and to see good benefits are all spiritually manoeuvred. Your attitude to life is subjugated on you by spiritual forces; if they be not unclean spirits, then the Holy Spirit must be.

God wants to be in charge of humans, but unbelief is stealing their hearts from their Creator.

"For this people's heart is waxed gross, and their ears are dull of hearing, and their eyes they have closed; lest at any time they should see with their eyes and hear with their ears, and should understand with their heart, and should be converted, and I should heal them." (Matthew 13:15).

What are highlighted in the above verse may seem to be tendencies engendered by flesh or bodily inclination of persons in their own making not to see their God. Though as true as they appeared to be, their behaviours were not spontaneous. They are impelled by powers beyond their control. They need to be saved; in other words, they will fight unbelief to get saved: for unbelief is a tragedy! And unbelief is not a measure for Christ Kingdom alone, but humans' blindness toward divine provisions. All that humans live to see, and experience, and withstand are by the longsuffering grace of God who they are unwilling to yield their earthly existence to. Can you really remember this?

> *"...and the LORD said in his heart, I will not again curse the ground any more for man's sake; for the imagination of man's heart is evil from his youth; neither will I again smite any more every thing living, as I have done. While the earth remaineth, seedtime and harvest, and cold and heat, and summer and winter, and day and night shall not cease," (Genesis 8:21-22).*

> *"And the LORD passed by before him (**Moses**,) and proclaimed, The LORD, The LORD God, merciful and gracious, **LONGSUFFERING** and abundant in goodness and truth..." (Read Exodus 34:5-7).*

The longsuffering of God enabled all things necessary for sustenance of humans' existence – seedtime and harvest, and cold and heat, and winter and summer, and day and night – altogether reveals his longsuffering which without the human race could be due for extermination.

Have you come closely to why our Lord Jesus said that unbelief deserves reproving? He told his disciples that when the Comforter, the Spirit of truth would come to represent him, he will reprove the world of sin, and of righteousness, and of judgment; and of sin, because they believe not on him, (Read John 16:7-11).

*"Or despises thou the riches of his goodness and forbearance and **longsuffering**; not knowing that the goodness of God leadeth thee to repentance? But after thy hardness and impenitent heart treasurest up unto thyself wrath against the day of wrath and revelation of the righteous judgment of God," (Romans 2:4-5).*

Now, I say unbelief is tragic; and whoever remains with it is ruining his life suffering a great loss. In all divine things, he or she is behind; whether rich or poor, not believing God is that he or she believes not in His life. Unbelief unknowingly belies all human woes, and had ruined many lives; from fearfulness to depressiveness, and from indulgence to hypocrisy. ***Therefore, if you don't deal with unbelief you will have all these to deal with:***

1. Fearfulness:

Fear is a gruesome syndrome occurring as impulses over times and reducing self-confidence without doubts that it's gradually discomfiting its victim. But you end up seeing yourself at its fullness becoming traumatic at every hopeless situation. You might judge yourself wrongly thinking you exist without support forces around you.

Think well! Can't you see you are just self-conceited? Mark out this. A man wise only in his own eye is worse than a fool. Perhaps you have been so because of the working of unbelief in you. Unbelief creates self-conceit in humans. They think life opens up to them what it has to offer; not necessarily because of some powers adduce to it.

"Seest thou a man wise in his own conceit? there is more hope of a fool than of him", (Proverbs 26:12).

Some people don't know that their fears come and stay because of unbelief. Even then, their fears started because of unbelief. And they keep on managing these fears as though they can contain them. See how it started:

> *"Because I called, and ye refused; I have stretched out my hand, and no man regarded; but ye have set at nought all my counsel, and would none of my reproof: I also will laugh at your calamity; I will mock when your fear cometh; when your fear cometh as desolation, and your destruction cometh as a whirlwind; when distress and anguish cometh upon you. Then shall they call upon me, but I will not answer; they shall seek me early, but they shall not find me," (Proverbs 1:24-28).*

When unbelief breeds fear, God steps aside if trouble hits a person who had not believed. Losses of any kind are possible when he or she lives believing not in God: for the test of believing God is one's fervent worshipping and trusting Him for grace. Don't call him or her unbeliever because there are many believers who exercise unbelief in maximum level. What is a man in unbelief? He is a fool above the fools! It's not my words; you read them: *"...there is more hope of a fool than of him."*

Calamities walk along with unbelieving people, taking them one day to another; sparing them no evil times. They fall sick under spiritual attacks; and make losses under spiritual attacks; and the devils among them know their kinds in the spiritual world to be vulnerable to afflictions. They suffer what ordinarily they would not have suffered if sustaining grace follows them; and they die when death wouldn't kill them, and suffer setback when prosperity would have come. They know their fears but have no wisdom to rid their fears off them.

> *"Doth not their excellency which is in them go away? They die, even without wisdom, (Job 4:21).*

Have you ever seen those who manifest unbelief? Have you seen their woes? Spiritual insensitivity had filled their hearts to the extent that they thought the fears that gripped them were just supply of life woes – either man will see it good or see it bad, so they thought and remained in unbelief. But they have seen those following God and witnessing miracles because they trusted Him. To them, all things divine are nonsense and allusions. Yet their fears are their doom. Unbelief! Yet the book of Psalm 91:1-6 speaks for every man who believes in the LORD God, saying:

"He that dwelleth in the secret place of the most High shall abide under the shadow of the Almighty. I will say of the LORD, He is my refuge and my fortress: my God; in him will I trust. Surely he shall deliver thee from the snare of the fowler, and from the noisome pestilence. He shall cover thee with his feathers, and under his wings shall thou trust: his truth shall be thy shield and buckler. Thou shalt not be afraid for the terror by night; nor for the arrow that flieth by day; nor for the pestilence that walketh in darkness; nor for the destruction that wasteth at noonday…"

Therefore believe to the saving of your soul: for sufficient for the day is the evil thereof, (Matthew 6:33-34).

2. Depressiveness:

Well, I do not wish anyone will ignore this symptom of unbelief. Depression is the state of the mind failing constantly to see anything enjoyable in life; a mind-set that lacks the ability to see reasons to be happy. Depression, if not controlled, will lead to sorrowfulness; and sorrow, when given a larger concern will lead to ill-health or speedy aging. The Psalmist had said:

"Why art thou cast down, O my soul? and why art thou disquieted within me? hope thou in God: for I shall yet praise him, who is the health of my countenance, and my God, (Psalm 42:11).

Wisdom was found in the above verse where there was hope in God; but unbelief does not permit any hope where God is missing. You are going to be dragged into disheartening condition with nothing in the universe to be trusted for help. In this I sympathise with anyone manifesting unbelief in his or her lifetime. Where will you find help if not of God? Why would you prevent yourself from seeing reality of grace from above? Unbelieving spirits are at work in you to give you the life you had never wished for.

For your information, life itself is more terrible than the devils we fear. Life's spells are accidental, and constant, supplying both good and evil situations which humans experience on daily basis.

"A man born of a woman is of few days, and full of trouble," (Job 14:1).

Do not say *'yes I know.'* You don't! And you can never know unless you're reasonably interested in your wellbeing: for a man who is interested in his wellbeing will know to trust in a deity, especially God; looking at the wondrous works of his hand.

"I will praise thee: for I am fearfully and wonderfully made: marvellous are thy works; and that my soul knoweth right well," (Psalm 139:14).

Does this verse make sense? It does! Should I continue in unbelieving lifestyle? Not good for me if I am in your shoes. Because he that fearfully and wonderfully made me deserves to have my heart trusting Him. Depressiveness will stop. But then, you are still unwilling to do so to overcome your unbelief. Jesus our Lord and Saviour expressed empathy on this, saying:

"It is the spirit that quickeneth; the flesh profiteth nothing: the words that I speak unto you, they are

60

spirit, and they are life. But there are some of you that believe not..." (John 6:63-64).

The words of the Lord are life-quickening spirits capable of restoring peace to your heart. I need them, and you too should let them into your soul. Jeremiah had said:

"Thy words were found, and I did eat them; and thy word was unto me the joy and rejoicing of mine heart: for I am called by thy name, O LORD God of hosts," (Jeremiah 15:16).

And Jesus, looking at the Devil eye balls to eye balls, overwhelmingly said in **Matthew 4:4** thus:

"It is written, Man shall not live by bread alone, but by every word that proceedeth out of the mouth of God."

Unbelieving lifestyle will deny a person the experience of life sustaining grace found in His words. The devils know your weakness. They help you think worse of life-stressing situations until life-quickening spirits are extinguished in you. You know what to expect, namely; frustration, hopelessness, and no-prayer lifestyle. You may likely get to a point of warring against your instincts.

"Therefore they say unto God, Depart from us; for we desire not the knowledge of thy ways. What is the Almighty that we should serve him? And what profit should we have, if we pray unto him?" (Job 21:14-15).

At the point anyone gets to these junctures, life meaning will be suppressed in his or her heart. Many melt down from the thick personalities to mere mortals and their positions on earth were not reckoned with; they vanished from the minds of people.

Also, there are those in attempts to sideline depression advertently became indulgent, and of them the world of men was driven into chaos. Those who wrongly solved depressive issues through indulgences had made the world of men unbearable. Unbelief! One's high way to damnation.

3. Indulgence:

Indulgence is the yielding of someone to temptations or desires likely seen by him or her as reliefs for depressive conditions. Such persons can steal, or sell themselves out in exchange for ameliorating offers they think can help their bad conditions. Some on the other hand had committed suicide; and some had taken others' life to feel the better. Some also ended up being useless to their societies, and practicing insolence was to them what people like them should be noted for.

Many on their own making had taken their indulgent tendencies to the heights of fraudulence to evade depressions which they think life offer. The world of men started tumbling from God's purpose to a desecrated world because of choices of humans whose hearts were far away from their Creator, God. Worsening situations were the results of unbelief seemingly unavoidable by humans.

Indulgent stage is the pathetic and self-craving moments of unbelieving lifestyle, leaving no place in one's life for recovery considering the facts that some by it went down the drains of life, and many by it turned out to become societal nuisance; and there are those who for fear of it chose the ways of criminality to attain heights of recognition in the world of men, taking advantage of a life without God to subdue possessions for themselves! Catch a world of men because of unbelieving lifestyles. Then there is this misinformed adage humans had chosen to apply to selves in order to find a platform for their miserable unbelieving lifestyles. You have heard people said: *'heaven will help those who help themselves.'* But the heaven you don't know will not help you!

Therefore unholy agents were birthed amongst the living: humans, both growing and matured individuals who see God's interventions in human existence as fiddles. These individuals were more interested in indulgences – worshipping of idols, ritualistic commitments, injurious attempts, subversions, culpable activities and various occult vices were pursued instead of submitting themselves to the will of their Creator. Up till now!

"And when they shall say unto you, Seek unto them that have familiar spirits, and unto wizards that peep, and that mutter: should not a people seek unto their God? for the living to the dead?" (Isaiah 8:19).

The powering unbelief had made the above counsel to men as fantasy not worth heeding. *If one must find his or her place on earth, let him or her pursue what makes heavenly life possible on earth before death comes* – so indulgent persons do think unto this day.

"For what shall it profit a man, if he shall gain the whole world and lose his own soul?" (Mark 8:36).

Likewise, indulgence instigated some to identify with religion houses, and they did enter not because they believed, but that unbelief and what it could achieve should be tied to testimonies which men considered to be of God! They remained in the domains of God to upsetting what are holy so that what are unholy will be tolerated – politics!

In a way, political settings originated from the unbelieving manoeuvres brought into the sanctuary of God by self-centred individuals who sought to tie what unbelieving activities had achieved to be equalled to testimonies of the Almighty. Humans' inclinations to the spiritual aspects of their lives were then based on what one had in possessions during one's time of existence as though such possessions whether gotten righteously or not were indications that God had reached him or her.

Hypocrisy started against the laws of the LORD God. *Don't ask questions, but seek answers in whatever ways that*

63

possessions are achievable on earth. These acts were very well appealing to the hearts of religion bigots.

Hypocrisy therefore sold the sanctuary to the world of men along with religious politics which unto this day are being practised to the detriments of purity and sanctity which are healthy living standards. Politics of unbelief were birthed from the sanctuary because of inability of humans to accept what *'will'* has God allowed for individuals who live believing on him and until now politics of hypocrites in the sanctuary of God are being used outside the sanctuary. Politics were firstly indeed noted to be hypocrisy and hypothesis. I will help you see that!

> *"Then spake Jesus to the multitude, and to his disciples, saying, The scribes and the Pharisees sit in Moses' seat: All therefore whatsoever they bid you observe, that observe and do; but do not ye after their works: for they say, and do not... But woe unto you, scribes and Pharisees, hypocrites! for ye shut the kingdom of heaven against men; for ye neither go in yourselves, neither suffer ye them that are entering to go in..."* **(Please read all Matthew 23).**

With time, mixture of humans' feelings concerning life matters degenerated to hypocritical undertakings, far from beholding the *'will'* of God for them which later turned out to be that people should be free to live with choices governed by their own acceptable norms regardless of calamities experienced in the management of unbelieving indulgent folks. Isn't that what politics allowed? And democracy (the government of the people, by the people, and for the people) became the last child of hypocrisy birthed for both the world of men and religion bigots. Unbelief! What world it has given! Inordinate desires filled the hearts of men to quench their thirst for sin which promote self-indulgences.

"For this cause God gave them up unto vile affections:
for even their women did change the natural use into

*that which is against nature (**lesbianism**): and likewise also the men, leaving the natural use of the woman, burned in their lust one toward another (**homosexuals**); men with men working that which is unseemly, and receiving in themselves that recompence of their error which was meet. And even as they did not like to retain God in their knowledge, God gave them over to a reprobate mind, to do those things which are not convenient;" (Romans 1:26-28).*

Why do people steal, cheat, subvert, and are corruptible? Isn't it because of lacking faith in God? Change anything in a person but you can hardly change his or her unbelieving lifestyles. A change does happen, yet in an uneasy way.

4. Hypocrisy:

All are indeed involved? And what is hypocrisy? Taking dictionary definition, hypocrisy means, *'the claim or pretence of holding beliefs, feelings, standards, qualities, opinions, virtues or motivations that one does not actually possess... applying criticism to others that one does not apply equally to oneself..."*

Isn't this fair definition, truly indicative of humans' behaviours? Man was created to live unto God from the beginning, but Satan twisted it in the hearts of the first couple, Adam and Even.

"And the serpent said unto the woman, Ye shall not surely die: for God doth know that in the day ye eat thereof, then your eyes shall be opened, and ye shall be as gods, knowing good and evil," (Genesis 3:4-5).

The above was a pretended demonstration of love by the serpent toward the woman, Eve, but wasn't done in sincerity of purpose. Unbelief was sown in the woman's heart and when the woman saw that the tree was good for food, and that it was pleasant to the eyes, and a tree to be desired to make one wise, she took of the fruit thereof, and did eat, and gave also to her husband with her; and he did eat. And their relatedness with God collapsed, and hypocrisy followed where each of them wanted to be right when unbelief was visible. The struggle to make the other wrong was paramount in their hearts. Apostle John therefore warned against lust:

> "I have written unto you, fathers, because ye have known him that is from the beginning. I have written unto you, young men, because ye are strong, and the word of God abideth in you, and ye have overcome the wicked one...
>
> "Love not the world, neither the things that are in the world. If any man love the world, the love of the Father is not in him. For all that is in the world, the lust of the flesh, and the lust of the eyes, and pride of life, is not of the Father, but is of the world...
>
> "And the world passeth away, and the lust thereof: but he that doeth the will of God abideth for ever," (1John 2:14-17).

Hold it! What started hypocrisy was lust in the hearts of men caused by their mind alertness, and for lust to have its ways among men; God's divine interventions in human matters were undermined. Then unbelief formed itself in those who saw God's interventions in humans' inordinate desires as very slow for their whims, even if it had been the 'will' of God that humans should trust him for their sojourning on earth. If not fears and depressions, indulgence and hypocrisy followed. So it became vibrant among humans to defend whatsoever they could indulge in doing through their unbelieving characteristics, and they sought for platforms where their doings could be tied to the testimonies of God.

The laws of God were undermined. Governments of men were then based on equal rights to choices as deserved by various nationalities. The consequences were that wickedness rose among humans because of unbelief and what it allowed. It was tribal problem. Unbelief was their sin and their damnation. It remained and stayed among humans, and birthed politics from within and outside the sanctuary. Priests blessed wickedness, and approved what indulgent men had gotten from unbelief. And Jesus hoped that the coming of the Holy Spirit will help men see their ways properly in the book of **John 16:8-14** which please read.

"And when he is come, he will reprove the world of sin, and of righteousness, and of judgment. Of sin, because they believe not on me;"

In this he spoke of unbelieving humans who see their sojourning on earth depended on what they possessed or achieved as self-prompted legendaries. Unbelief became the ultimate sin that has ruined the world of men onward to date.

"Of righteousness, because I go to my Father, and ye see me no more; Of judgment, because the prince of this world is judged."

Significantly, righteousness will connect you to heavenly realm where Jesus himself ascended after his sojourn on earth and the earth shall no more behold you: for though you are in the world you are not of the world. (Read all John 17).

Let it be known that the world had been freed on the Cross; yet, what unbelief had birthed has not been broken. It's telling on humans. Confusions everywhere we know. The end shall prove men wrong in all. The serpent by which sin was initiated was defeated on the Cross, and the word of God says as many that believed shall be saved. (Read Romans 10:1-13).

Chapter Five

GROWING YOUR SPIRITUAL LIFE

'Be doers of the word, and not hearers only, deceiving your own selves,' were good counsel by Apostle James to the Church.

If there be any man that God had to curse, or if there be any ugly citation in the Holy Bible where God issued a curse upon men, it had been directed unto the hearers who refused to do what the law of God encapsulated. If there be anything referred to as provocation of the LORD God, it had been unto arrogant and nonchalant individuals. And we all as well know that arrogance is not only despising sacred knowledge but also ignoring what such knowledge offered which makes an arrogant person as a nonchalant individual. May you never be a hearer only but also a doer of the word in the name of Jesus! Amen!!

Instruct a friend, or a child, or a servant and find out if he has instincts to grow his spiritual existence when he either chooses or ignores to apply good counsel that deserves obeying.

In concluding of that verse; we sight *'deceiving your own selves.'*

Now, let's test the wisdom of the Apostle who authored the counsel. In ages behind us, he wrote for our admonition. Why was he thinking about you who must hear the word and also be a doer? Saying, if you heard the word and did not perform it, you were deceiving your own selves! What wisdom did the Apostle develop? Any man who understands the spiritual and is close to God, and looking unto God while he expends his life on earth may not be a hearer who does not perform what he hears of the word of God. You may deceive your own self by pretention, when you want others to see that you are actually on the right path. Perhaps, you're comfortable with pretence! But can pretence ever makes a man real? I don't think so; not in this!

68

Sometimes, I wonder how come one joined himself to a Church of God, having a priest over him; involves in prayers with which he could say, '*amen*,' and yet does not plan to grow himself and the house of God, but rather he indulges himself in nonchalant acts in defiance of good counsel from the word of God that should grow his spiritual life and his Church inclusive.

We see many Christians lack this understanding: that the place where they believed to have their spiritual life in control should grow as well as their own life. We see those who the only thing they are concerned with is that every insightful word spoken by their priests in prayer which they can quickly claim with '*amen*' must come to be fulfilled in their lives which at many occasions such does not happen as they hoped it would. Do you know why? I think they are exercising folly on things that are spiritual.

In the case of a Christian; he has the Bible, and he has a Church with a name; which he professes anywhere he goes, but he is unwilling to be born-again by the word, deceiving his own self. What do you say about such setback in spiritual pursuits?

Again, who are others who deceive themselves? The fools! A fool has eyes but he cannot see what are spiritual with them, (1Corinthians 2:14). He has a heart that cannot perceive wisdom: for he's an arguer, but for his whims and caprices only. He has ears that would not hear what are outside his impulse. Not always seeing that he has become a fool, he argues that the light the sun offers suffices for the light the word of God called for. Instead of seeing the light of wisdom, he walks in his physical sights which most likely are closer things to him. Tell him to eschew darkness, he sees you as an agitator who had developed into eccentric. Haven't you seen such man if you're not exactly one?

Hear me: when I gave my life to Christ I began to see those who walk in darkness. But before then, I had argued that what I knew and what I could reach were all about life and one's tranquillity. I had lied to myself until the days when I started indulging in performance of God's word. I entered into another world before I knew it; a world far off from many kings and princes. It is a world of the spiritual where things are just

69

accurate and provable. God is there! I started growing in the knowledge of all wisdom and divine attitude. The things that are true, honest, just, pure, lovely, and all things that are of good report formed my life each day I was seeing, (Philippians 4:8). Even now I am still trying for more.

For you, if you have not amended your cravings to do what the word of God says, you may not find the world that I have known. Its glory is awesome as of that only allowed by God Himself. In my world, there are no pains without hope and solution. I have found a better option to life crises; my soul found prosperity, and good health, and I have prospered in the knowledge of the spiritual.

Therefore, do not be a hearer only but also a doer of God's word. There is gain in it. (James 1:22-25; 3John 1:2). Do not always forget what you have been told to achieve by the word of God – to hear and to perform. Now, let's walk on the pathways by which one grows his spiritual life steadily as expounded in **Philippians 4:8-9.**

> *"Finally, brethren, whatsoever things are true, whatsoever things are honest, whatsoever things are just, whatsoever things are pure, whatsoever things are lovely, whatsoever things are of good report; if there be any virtue, and if there be any praise, think on these things. Those things, which ye have both learned, and received, and heard, and seen in me, do: and the God of peace shall be with you,"*

These are proofs of excellence in a modest follower of the Lord; things drawn from learning, embraced when heard; and expected to be seen in our attitude in the midst of others. Apostle Paul had once professed these facts this way:

> *"Providing for honest things, not only in the sight of the Lord, but also in the sight of men,"* *(2Corinthians 8:21).*

Be a Christian who is determined to grow spiritually and also determined to support your local church growing efforts thus:

1. Whatsoever Things are true assigned!

It's always better to place sincere attitude as an assignment if one must pursue to achieve a blameless lifestyle before God and others. For Apostle Paul to have to say, *'think on these things'*, has indicated them to be assignments which must be pursued. There is no reason seeing yourself as a Christian when you cannot afford to conduct yourself in what makes Christianity true in the sight of the Almighty and also men of this world.

> *"But the hour cometh, and now is, when the true worshippers shall worship the Father in spirit and in truth: for the Father seeketh such to worship him,"* *(John 4:23).*

This is significant to true worshippers of God and it's not negotiable. I have spoken in a previous chapter (*Hidden Strength*) on how one can attain to spiritual living by intuitiveness of what the LORD is in spiritual relationship with mankind. That is worshipping God in spirit; but to adapt to worshipping God in truth has to do with one's ability to abundantly submit himself to irresistible acts that promote the gathering of God's people irrespective of your weakness, or status, or endeavours.

There are irresistible acts as laid down for the kingdom of Christ that one cannot harden his or her heart against, because they are assignments before us which if we pursue to achieve them we are seen as worshipping the LORD in truth.

> *"And he (Jesus) said unto them, Go ye into all the world, and preach the gospel to every creature,"* *(Mark 16:15).*

"And let us consider one another to provoke unto love and to good works: not forsaking the assembling of ourselves together, as the manner of some is..." (Hebrews 10:24-25).

"Bring ye all the tithes into the storehouse, that there may be meat in mine house..." (Malachi 3:10).

"The woman shall not wear that which pertaineth unto a man, neither shall a man put on a woman's garment: for all that do so are abomination unto the LORD thy God," (Deuteronomy 22:5).

"But every woman that prayeth or prophesieth with her head uncovered dishonoureth her head: for that is even all one as if she were shaven," (1Corinthians 11:5).

"And so he that had received five talents came and brought other five talents, saying, lord, thou deliveredst unto me five talents: behold, I have gained beside them five talents more. His lord said unto him, well done, thou good and faithful servant: thou hast been faithful over a few things, I will make thee ruler over many things: enter thou into the joy of thy lord," (Matthew 25:20-21).

With these few verses one should be able to identify what are irresistible acts which must be pursued while he or she follows the Lord. It is a duty on Christians to be sincere to the call of God. And Joshua had solicited, saying:

"Now therefore fear the LORD, and serve him in sincerity and in truth..." (Joshua 24;14).

When sincerity and truth are not observed on one's part, then he or she is seen as a hypocrite. Therefore acquaint yourself to things that are true without arguments and you would have developed the fruit of the Spirit and you're spiritual.

2. Whatsoever Things are honest assigned!

Be honest with yourself! Do you really want to be part of the kingdom? If yes, then be honest with yourself first. Are you willing to be upright in your lifetime with the Lord? Are you going to be cleared when the Lord returns, or perhaps when you're expected to defend your stand as a Christian?

> *"For if we sin wilfully after that we have received the knowledge of the truth, there remaineth no more sacrifice for sins, but a certain fearful looking for of judgment and fiery indignation, which shall devour the adversaries," (Hebrews 10:26-27).*

Not many can assess their own self's honesty in many things they have given themselves to do, especially brethren in the kingdom of Christ. Being honest is projecting your identity prominently to make men and even devils know where you belong. There are borders already; and if you don't know them, the people that watch you know them. And what do they think about you when you're not reliable?

> *"Blessed is the man that walketh not in the counsel of the ungodly, nor standeth in the way of sinners, nor sitteth in the seat of the scornful. But his delight is in the law of the LORD; and in his law doth he meditate day and night," (Psalms 1:1-2).*

> *"Be ye not unequally yoked together with unbelievers: for what fellowship hath righteousness with unrighteousness? and what communion hath light with darkness?" (2 Corinthians 6:14).*

"This book of the law shall not depart out of thy mouth; but thou shalt meditate therein day and night, that thou mayest observe to do according to all that is written therein: for then thou shalt make thy way prosperous, and then thou shalt have good success," (Joshua 1:8).

"Wherefore seeing we also are compassed about with so great a cloud of witnesses, let us lay aside every weight, and the sin which doth so easily beset us, and let us run with patience the race that is set before us," (Hebrews 12:1).

The Scripture is a mirror that is able to put to test one's honesty to himself and God. To grow spiritually depends on how you view yourself in scriptural mirrors. I mean your equation with Biblical assertions. Let them reform you; and that's when you can discreetly say you are honest to the call. Apostle Paul said, *think on these things!*

3. Whatsoever Things are just assigned!

A balance relationship with all is still a better evidence of spiritual development. Be equitable to others. Don't be covetous in your doings. Cheating on others is exactness of being wise in your own conceits which is not a fair dealing with them.

"Be of the same mind one toward another. Mind not high things, but condescend to men of low estate. Be not wise in your own conceits," (Romans 12:16).

When you deceived people, you have rubbished your Christian identity before others. Don't pride over them either. You're inexcusable to become unjust person in the church of God. Not even in business dealings you are justified to be unfair to the other. Even in judging between two or more others, you

74

must be fair to all of them not being partial. And don't bear false witness because you chose to take side with someone you want to favour.

> *"For they that are such serve not our Lord Jesus Christ, but their own belly; and by good words and fair speeches deceive the hearts of the simple," (Romans 16:18).*

> *"Let me be weighed in an even balance that God may know mine integrity,"* Job had said, *(Job 31:6).*

> *"A false balance is abomination to the LORD, but a just weight is his delight," (Proverbs 11:1).*

> *"Divers weights are an abomination unto the LORD; and a false balance is not good," (Proverbs 20:23).*

Therefore, do not live as though life does not end somewhere: for whatsoever a man sows he shall reap. Be just in all things! Only then you're standing spiritually grown.

4. Whatsoever Things are pure assigned!

> *"Unto the pure all things are pure: but unto them that are defiled and unbelieving is nothing pure; but even their mind and conscience is defiled. They profess that they know God; but in works they deny him, being abominable, and disobedient, and unto every good work reprobate," (Titus 1:15-16).*

In this matter there are circumstances of the defiled humans that are noted as unbelieving ones; and it is also noted of them to have possessed critical hearts which though they profess that they know God; but they would not give themselves to obey his rules. Impurity is the state of the mind of anyone whose conscience does not see anything good order than what such person thinks of himself and chooses to do, whether be it immoral. Many are in the church and the church is not in them! Arousing offences is their first choice, and obscenities are their priorities. Are you one of them? Then gross darkness has come upon you!

The church of Christ is a refining home where individuals receive in themselves the pattern of lifestyles ordained by God for his people, (Isaiah 43:21). Spiritual growth is not the heap of Bible translations you have around you but the evidence of Christ-like traits you expedite on. It is not the prayerful mood you bear on your face but the evidence of Christ motivated freedom working in you. Your spiritual growth has nothing to do with the environments you find yourself, but how you influence such environments to experience the world you found as a Christian.

*"I beseech you therefore, brethren, by the mercies of God, that ye present your bodies a living sacrifice, holy, acceptable unto God, which is your reasonable service. And be not conformed to this world: but be ye transformed by the renewing of your mind, that ye may prove what is that good, and acceptable, and perfect, will of God, (**Read Romans 12:1-21**).*

If your enemy is hungry or thirsty, have you tried to feed and give him to drink? Have you overcome evil with good? When have you held back yourself from vengeance or malice when someone hurt you? How have you laboured to ensure you dwell peaceably with all men?

"Recompense to no man evil for evil. Provide things honest in the sight of all men, (Romans 12:17).

Do you know that a pure heart does not consider offences and all attitudinal demonstrations are without a consequential return to anyone who he or she knows is unsanctified in the knowledge of God? Defiled persons surround us at homes and local churches; but they are ever learning and not able to come to the knowledge of truth. And to say you're growing spiritually is to be able to tolerate them even when they refuse your gestures; because they can't really serve the Lord either. They are abominable, and disobedient, and deny the Lord every essential effort they could offer. We know them; but they should not know us in conformity to their ways. Here I say, always love them the way they are in conformity with these verses.

"Ye are of God, little children, and have overcome them: because greater is he that is in you, than he that is in the world...and we have known and believed the love that God hath to us. God is love; and he that dwelleth in love dwelleth in God, and God in him... If a man say, I love God, and hateth his brother, he is a liar: for he that loveth not his brother whom he hath seen, how can he love God whom he hath not seen," (1 John 4:4, 16, 20).

5. Whatsoever Things are lovely assigned!

"Then Jesus saith unto them, Children, have ye any meat? They answered him, No. And he said unto them, Cast the net on the right side of the ship, and ye shall find. They cast therefore, and now they were not able to draw it for the multitude of fishes. Therefore that disciple whom Jesus loved saith unto Peter, It is the Lord...

*"As soon then as they were come to land, they saw a fire of coals there, and fish laid thereon, and bread. Jesus saith unto them, Bring of the fish which ye have now caught... Jesus saith unto them, Come and dine. And none of the disciples durst ask him, Who art thou? knowing that it was the Lord, " (**Read John 21:4-12**).*

This act as simple as it looks is a lovely disposition of someone who cares for others. Our Lord Jesus' caring behaviours are expected to be part of our life as Christians. Oh yes, he once laid aside his garment and washed his disciples' feet; and also had fed five thousand in a lovely manner, (John 13:1-5; 6:1-13).

These events were lovely to the hearts that heard them done by the Lord Jesus unto men. They make sense of lovely attitude toward others around him. He gave a parable about when he was hungry and certain people gave him no food, and thirsty but they gave no drink; and he was a stranger, and they did not host him; and was naked, and they clothed him not. Then the people answered him, questioning when did they see him hungry, or thirsty, or a stranger, or naked, or sick, or in prison, and did not minister to him? And the Lord answered them, saying:

> *"...verily I say unto you, inasmuch as ye did it not to one of the least of these, ye did it not to me,"* **(Read Matthew 25:31-46)**.

For a Christian to be lovely around his neighbourhood or in his local church he must be readily available to dispense goods and services to all around him. **Being generous is being lovely**. Job was! He tried in his days to do all that were lovely in the sight of men.

> *"I put on righteousness, and it clothed me: my judgment was as a robe and a diadem. I was eyes to the blind, and feet was I to the lame. I was a father to the poor; and the cause which I knew not I searched out,"* *(Job 29:14-17)*.

Dorcas was a woman seen as too lovely to die in her time. It was written of her: *"...this woman was full of good works and almsdeeds which she did,* **(Read Acts 9:36-42)**.

And we also learnt of the souls won in the early church because of lovely deeds in common among them.

"Neither was there any among them that lacked: for as many as were possessors of lands or houses sold them, and brought the prices of the things that were sold, and laid them down at the apostles' feet: and distribution was made unto every man according as he had need, (Acts 4:34-35).

I am not careful about this section because it's now being practiced hypocritically among Christians. Some don't even see reasons for outreach services and cares. It does not need your local church involvement to make you one lovely Christian among many. Growing spiritually is inclusive of your generosity to all around you: for this is lovely. Now, I say, *think on these things.* If you will not, one part of your spiritual life is plucked off! Certainly!

6. Whatsoever Things are of good report assigned!

Good report of anyone is exactly his or her spiritual assuredness. You have to build on having your behaviours being spoken about with respect from others. You deserve it when you have successfully performed the above reforms.

"Let your moderation be known unto all men. The Lord is at hand," (Philippians 4:5).

What is well spoken of about someone is what he has done well in respect to what he shows he is before others. You are God's representative on earth. You must present godliness that cannot be faulted. This way one draws a good grace to himself and finds peace in his heart.

However, Apostle Paul indicated that these reforms can only be an assuredness of spiritual posture if there be any virtue, and if there be any praise attached to them. Here I see virtue and praise as two apposite dimensions in evaluating how sincere one is in what he or she is doing in drawing attention to his or her

79

spiritual attainment and what must be observed of them. The efficacy of what a Christian makes others to observe is then based on how mindful is he or she of the word of God when applied to view his behaviours. Praise has been achieved by many and virtue is yet to be seen in what they're doing which has drawn good report from the societies they belong. I mean some aggrandized and self-serving, and pious individuals in the Church of Christ who only are mindful of how they would deceive men to observe all these reforms in them when they have not achieved them on the platform of God's word. Could it be that the Psalmist witnessed such individuals in his days?

"Hear this, all ye people; give ear, all ye inhabitants of the world: both low and high, rich and poor, together. My mouth shall speak of wisdom; and the meditation of my heart shall be of understanding...

"I will incline mine ear to a parable: I will open my *dark saying upon the harp. Wherefore should I fear in the days of evil, when the iniquity of my heels shall compass me about? They that trust in their wealth, and boast themselves in the multitude of their riches; none of them can by any means redeem his brother, nor give to God a ransom for him: (for the redemption of their soul is precious, and it ceaseth for ever:) that he should still live for ever, and not see corruption...*

"For he seeth that wise men die, likewise the fool and the brutish person perish, and leave their wealth to others. Their inward thought is, that their houses shall continue for ever, and their dwelling places to all generations; they call their lands after their own names. Nevertheless man being in honour abideth not: he is like the beasts that perish. This their way is their folly: yet their posterity approve their sayings. Selah...

"Like sheep they are laid in the grave; death shall feed on them; and the upright shall have dominion over them in the morning; and their beauty shall consume in the grave from their dwelling. But God will redeem my soul from the power of the grave: for he shall receive me. Selah...

*"Be not thou afraid when one is made rich, when the glory of his house is increased; for when he dieth he shall carry nothing away: his glory shall not descend after him. Though **while he lived he blessed his soul: and men will praise thee, when thou doest well to thyself**...*

"He shall go to the generation of his fathers; they shall never see light. Man that is in honour, and understandeth not, is like the beasts that perish," (Psalms 49).

But I know there is no condemnation to them which are in Christ Jesus, who walk not after the flesh, but after the Spirit of God: for the law of the Spirit of life in Christ Jesus has made us free from the law of sin and death, (Romans 8:1-2).

Spiritual growth is not self-centred praises but virtuousness. May you grow well in the Spirit! Amen!

Chapter Six

FOR A QUIET TIME

Have you thought about spending a quiet time with God? A quiet time is when all feelings and emotional traumas are dropped, and the heart is given a chance to experience quietness. In such instance you just want to be liberated from life issues and desires, but at the same time need a companion; nobody else but God your Creator. This time, not necessarily going to a mountain top to be away from people, but to allow a quiet state of your heart and avoid what it offers; and also freed from all the activities of the day. Is it really possible? you may ask. But in the presence of God, there is fullness of joy.

To spend time with your Creator with all lined up activities of the day is near impossible, but you've to work it out and expedite on it and believe it. Hear me out! The nearest devil to you (*your mind*) is always too inclined to activities requiring your attention throughout the day that you're overstretched to think about a quiet time with God. But you need it! To hell with whatever you have to do! Satan is at a closer range to your mind and he knows the implications of letting you close to God, so he keeps your mind on many things awaiting your attention; and most of them are duties unending!

As a Christian, you need a worthwhile moment with God and for you to study his words, and to eat them: for man rarely live a comforted lifetime without every word that proceeds out of the mouth of the Almighty, (Matthew 4:4). Jeremiah buttressed it!

"Thy words were found, and I did eat them, and thy word was unto me the joy and rejoicing of mine heart: for I am called by thy name, O LORD God of hosts," *(Jeremiah 15:16).*

82

This is a helpful assertion by Jeremiah who hungered to search for His words, and when he found His words he did consume them which in turn reformed his state of mind to joying and rejoicing and knowing that he was a product of God. There should not be setback to this reforming mission daily with the Lord. A quiet time is when you stay alone, in quietness of the mind, only desiring to be filled with the grace of righteousness.

"Blessed are they which do hunger and thirst after righteousness: for they shall be filled," (Matthew 5:6)

.   Do not let your body be unduly accustomed to labouring, burden bearing, inordinate desiring, and heaviness of the heart all day long without seizing even an hour to enter into the Palace of God. I see the Bible as the Palace of God which is soul-lifting enough for an individual to visit on daily basis the same way an earthly man who chooses to have a cordial relationship with his earthly king visits his palace daily to have a rapport with his king. Joshua was enjoined to do that by God himself.

"This book of the law shall not depart out of thy mouth; but thou shalt meditate therein day and night, that thou mayest observe to do according to all that is written therein: for then thou shalt make thy way prosperous, and then thou shalt have good success," (Joshua 1:8).

Ignore this, you will end up being retarded in many things and also have your divine progress stalled in life. But when one chooses to establish a divine relationship with the LORD God, he or she experiences the leading of the Holy Spirit who will usher him or her across His walls in all wisdom and spiritual understanding of His words; and this kind of experience pours comforting grace abundantly on one's soul: and such is very refreshing and prompting to spiritual living.

*"But the Comforter, which is the Holy Ghost, whom
the Father will send in my name, he shall teach you all
things, and bring all things to your remembrance,
whatsoever I have said unto you," (John 14:26).*

Then, experience your journey on earth applying what I
call the FOUR WHEELS for victory which are: **hope, faith,
grace, and patience.**

1. Hope in view:

Hope will foretell your future. Being hopeful is an
indicative of one's future and what it holds for him or her
becoming realistic in due time; and hope itself is the belief that
something wished for can or will happen. And the actualizing of
hope is anchored on the relationship one has developed with the
Lord based on high level meditation on the word of God.

*"But his delight is in the law of the LORD; and in his
law doth he meditate day and night. And he shall be
like a tree planted by the rivers of water, that bringeth
forth his fruit in his season; his leaf also shall not
wither; and whatsoever he doeth shall prosper,"
(Psalms 1:2-3).*

*"And hope maketh not ashamed; because the love of
God is shed abroad in our hearts by the Holy Ghost
which is given unto us," (Romans 5:5).*

Certainly, hope supported by the word of God guarantees
one's future. Do not attempt to form hope within you without the
supportiveness of his word: for you may live on not achieving a
blissful future, unless there are no longer devils. But you and I
know they are there to hinder and to break down blessings.

"For they sleep not, except they have done mischief; and their sleep is taken away, unless they cause some to fall," (Proverbs 4:16).

However, we do have many who overtake hopefulness with occultism, seeking help from observers of times, or diviners, or consulters with familiar spirits; which you must not do, (Deuteronomy 18:10-12). In any situation, protect your hope from your stressful state of mind: for hope is useless where faith fails.

2. Faith in view:

Faith takes what does not actually present itself physically from where it is hidden in the spiritual world, or demands for it to manifest, either by enforcing, influencing, and judging to make room for it to manifest. Faith is not the fanaticism people put forth for the pride of what they do or achieve of God which even they know not the sources of their manifestation, and if it reached fanaticism we know that obsessive behaviour has crept in and gotten its holds on the practice of faith. And obsession is an indicative involvement of Satanism which many individuals are doing. Such persons are no more in faith.

"Now faith is the substance of things hoped for, the evidence of things not seen... but without faith it is impossible to please him: for he that cometh to God must believe that he is, and that he is a rewarder of them that diligently seek him," (Hebrews 11:1, 6).

I will deal with this with intent to see you have pure faith in God so that your hope becomes realistic in due time. If you are mindful of yourself, you will realize that hope of future has formed expectations in you, whether those things expected are sure or sourceless in contemporary. Then if only you can adjust your mind to seeing them happening as well in the time looked to; and even if the time arrived and your expectations have not happened, wait patiently. And if only you can also continue to intuit that you deserve them and that with God they shall materialize in miracle forms. Inspire yourself further to deal with certain occurrences of challenges that keep coming up to reduce the impact you have developed concerning what you expected. Keep on rejoicing in the Lord against all odds and fail not to intuit that your future is in his hand – this is an enforcement of your faith! Then influence your assurance thus:

> *"Casting down imaginations, and every high thing that exalteth itself against the knowledge of God, and bringing into captivity every thought to the obedience of Christ; and having in a readiness to revenge all disobedience, when your obedience is fulfilled," (2 Corinthians 10:5-6).*

On this course, be ready in prayer to judge all obstacles propping their heads against the will of God for you – this is yoke-breaking that determines what you have chosen to attain in life. Sustain your faith with more hopeful things awaiting you. You will get there! I say you will get there! It is a mountain that you're ascending, but a molehill due trampling down!

> *"For I reckon that the sufferings of this present time are not worthy to be compared with the glory which shall be revealed in us. For the earnest expectation of the creature waiteth for the manifestation of the sons of God. For the creature was made subject to vanity, not willingly, but by reason of him who hath subjected the same in hope," (Romans 8:18-20).*

Therefore, you must have to stand tall and visible against all odds, and let your spirits swelling intensively in expectation bring to past what you hoped for, most times not like exactly what you designed in your heart. In this God beats us to it: for he recognizes the labour of your faith, but He proves the resolute of his majesty in all things that one believes him for to do! God comes up in his own way, but faith gives you your expectations! So faith will take hold of your future when you have it.

"And we know that all things work together for good to them that love God, to them who are the called according to his purpose," (Romans 8:28).

3. Grace in view:

Grace will preserve you for upcoming future. Preachers keep on saying grace is an unmerited favour of God. They are right, but such grace is the LORD's **longsuffering grace** negotiated on Noah in his days till the end of the world, (Genesis 8:20-22). Longsuffering grace sustains all the living until now even in the case of their sinfulness, but there is grace that specially holds His people; I mean those who believe in Him and become His people. God is the Creator of all humans sustained by his longsuffering grace, but not the Father of all, (Read 2 Corinthians 6:14-18). And also do reason with this scripture.

"Behold, the eye of the LORD is upon them that fear him, upon them that hope in his mercy; to deliver their soul from death, and to keep them alive in famine. Our soul waiteth for the LORD: he is our help and our shield. For our heart shall rejoice in him, because we have trusted in his holy name. Let thy mercy, O LORD, be upon us, according as we hope in thee," (Psalms 33:18-22).

This is the special grace to be seen as the love of God to them who look up to him and are called by his name. We are! Longsuffering grace is different from grace of mercy which believers enjoy. Believers are the ones that this grace applies to on their journey on earth. Believers are the LORD's people. But then, we are enjoined to therein work out our salvation in earnest composure.

> *"If my people, which are called by my name, shall humble themselves, and pray, and seek my face, and turn from their wicked ways; then will I hear from heaven, and will forgive their sin, and will heal their land. Now mine eyes shall be open, and mine ears attent unto the prayer that is made in this place," (2 Chronicles 7:14-15).*

Here we are: we got special grace to live on with when our obedience is fulfilled. We are born of God and we have this grace to overcome and conquer all obstacles and remain blessed. Our expectations cannot be cut short because we have a Father above.

> *"For whatsoever is born of God overcometh the world: and this is the victory that overcometh the world, even our faith," (1 John 5:4).*

Halleluiah, praise be to the Lord. His covering for us is sure, and all-inspiring. What will weaken us has been dealt with under special grace; we are preserved to see a future ordained by Him no matter the level of obstacles we experience daily.

> *"Likewise the Spirit also helpeth our infirmities: for we know not what we should pray for as we ought: but the Spirit itself maketh intercession for us with groanings which cannot be uttered," (Romans 8:26).*

> *"Ask, and it shall be given you; seek, and ye shall find; knock, and it shall be opened unto you: for every one that asketh receiveth; and he that seeketh findeth; and to him that knocketh it shall be opened. Or what man is there of you, whom if his son ask bread, will he give him a stone? Or if he ask a fish, will he give him a*

serpent? If ye then, being evil, know how to give good gifts unto your children, how much more shall your Father which is in heaven give good things to them that ask him?" (Matthew 7:7-11).

Oh, haven't you a Father in heaven? He is there arms opened to embrace you into his fold. His grace is sufficient for us, and his strength has made us perfect in weakness. However, know that grace is unfruitful when patience fails?

4. Patience in view:

"For we are saved by hope: but hope that is seen is not hope: for what a man seeth, why doth he yet hope for? But if we hope for that we see not, then do we with patience wait for it," (Romans 8:24-25).

Impatience can screw hope off you. While patience is the surging ability continually rising in a believer to wait patiently under all circumstances for a change of situations, impatience causes restlessness mostly at a time when one seemingly is under pressure to see certain hope comes to reality. The journey in life itself is crooked as hills, or valleys, or mountains, to go through; and with grace you might have it blissful for a season likewise.

*"To every thing there is a season, and a time to every purpose under the heaven... a time to weep, and a time to laugh; a time to mourn, and a time to dance... a time to get, and a time to lose... I have seen the travail, which God hath given to the sons of men to be exercised in it," **(Read Ecclesiastes 3:1-10)**.*

Patience should not be undermined in one's journey on earth and as followers of God, be rest assured that his eye is upon them that hope in his mercies. The death of Jesus Christ on the Cross was not a waste of purpose; and should not be eroded in one's heart by passion for certain earthly materials which can pass away even when we have them. A quiet time with God is urgently necessary in one's life which enables him or her to adjust from grim feelings and emotional traumas. All men have seen evil, denial, frustration, and whatever that humbled them to think more of God's help. Some challenges enforce faith if there be fellowship before then. If there be no genuine fellowship then such individuals need to be helped with proposing counsel which likely will establish some amount of faith in them.

> *"Therefore being justified by faith, we have peace with God through our Lord Jesus Christ: by whom also we have access by faith into* **this grace wherein we stand***, and rejoice in hope of the glory of God…*

> *"And not only so, but we glory in tribulations also: knowing that tribulation worketh patience; and patience, experience; and experience, hope: and hope maketh not ashamed: because the love of God is shed abroad in our hearts by the Holy Ghost which is given unto us. For when we were yet without strength, in due time Christ died for the ungodly," (Romans 5:1-6).*

Patience is a self-prompted gift when you exercise it all through a time of grim realities. Job outsuffered anyone ever known. He lost all material things and suffered ill-health along with – no children; and no material things to have to look onto, and yet his ailment became his hell. All circumstances that men must experience on earth were made clearer by him, saying:

> *"Man that is born of a woman is of few days, and full of trouble. He cometh forth like a flower, and is cut down: he fleeth also as a shadow, and continueth not…For there is hope of a tree, if it be cut down, that it will sprout again, and that the tender branch thereof will not cease…*

"Though the root thereof wax old in the earth, and the stock thereof die in the ground; yet through the scent of water it will bud, and bring forth boughs like a plant...

"If a man die, shall he live again? All the days of my appointed time will I wait, till my change come," (Read Job 14:1-14).

'***Through the scent of water***' is like the provision of grace which God ever supply to men. Though, your condition had tampered with your sure faith in God, grace for realities will soon come if only you know to exercise patience. A quiet time! Yeah!

And victory depends on these FOUR WHEELS and upon them it springs forth. If you cannot find them inside you after spending time (no matter how long with God,) then victory will stay back as if though there is no God! Have you ever helped yourself in this wise? I pray now with the unction of grace upon you; that you are not destined to fail under ugly experience... you will overcome in the mighty name of Jesus! Amen!

Chapter Seven

THE VEIL OF DESTINY

Destiny is a complex vehicle all humans drive in daily and it's seen as unable to change from what it has pasted on man; so let us say it's a veil. Like a vehicle on motion in a clumsy roadway and the driver behind the steering wheel manoeuvring – a little to the right and to the left, or haply a slide off the roadway; then a crash! And a journey is accomplished, if not a safe journey, it should be a crashed one – so is destiny! A clumsy roadway!

Our whim and caprice are like the steering mechanism that propels one's destiny. A sudden desire or change of mind; or a sudden change of mood or behaviour will predetermine what will happen to someone in present time and future which men call destiny. Also, he was abandoned too early in life; or not being cared for at teenage age; or he was stubborn and unredeemable; or there was too much inadequate desires when growing up; or unbelieving attitude toward his creator – just name as many as your spirit can help you do: then a *self-structured* world grew over and whelmed him – therefore his destiny formed! After all, a way that a man has chosen is his destiny; perhaps, wading off all what God had wished him because of self choices. And we know every way has its end reality. But how do I know God wished me well? You have to see God in his lovingkindness in your intuitions. He is faithful unlike a mortal man.

Self-will brings a man's own destiny upon him starting from childhood when he had begun to decide for self what choices he believes to be the priorities of his existence on earth; most likely because of upbringing, or environmental influences, or carefree lifestyles, or some other providence beyond one's control. But the starting point of one's destiny from infanthood is suspiciously foreordained and God can't be blamed for that either: because those parents from whom you came to life might have engaged themselves in self-will. Would you have asked God: why are *he and she* my parents?

People are given to believe that destiny of a man is constant and it is a hidden power believed to control what will happen to that man in present time and in the future with no indication of defeating it. But I know that gloomy destiny can be positively influenced, if not totally obliterated, where it's unfruitful and insecure, though people say it can't be dealt with because it is a condition foreordained by a power unknown to men. As true as it seemed believable, so also it could be one's own making of his or her destiny. In most cases, one can manage his or her destiny under all changes that might spring forth if he or she knows there is God; because destiny exhibits changes!

Get it right! God gets involved in man's life prophetically. And God controls human race with prophecies forespoken and what men do with His prophecies predetermines their destinies. Read for instance:

"For God so loved the world that he gave his only begotten Son, that whosoever believeth in him should not perish, but have everlasting life... He that believeth on him is not condemned: but he that believeth not is condemned already, because he hath not believed in the name of the only begotten Son of God," (John 3:16-18).

What you read is a prophecy supplied for one's destiny under the control of God and if you ignored it, then it is your destiny under your control. Therefore, God's prophetic provisions were meant to supply positive changes to one's destiny if he or she may view them with keen interests.

Come to think of it: prophecies from the Almighty are constant and endure forever; and humans' self-wishes for change are also constant but do not endure for too long. Both can relate adequately or inadequately depending on where the heart of a man is set, (Read Colossians 3:1-7). Changes wished for by a man working contrarily to God's prophecies will cause gross darkness, (Isaiah 60:2). And the destiny a man has structured out for himself is his fate, but a change channelled in the light of God's word is the destiny God has ordained for us all.

Do not jump to conclusion that the way I approach this subject makes destiny awkward. Destiny provides for what are good and what are evil as well. A keen conscious view of yourself will reveal times of different incidents occurring in your life; some are appealing, and some are unwanted, and some are tolerable, and some are questionable, and some are nerve-killing. You are wading in them all! None of them seemed planned for and they just happened, and they whelmed; and you're subjugated to experience what they provided for you. You are living a life of destiny; and destiny is a personal spell to everyone or nation – a clumsy roadway before all!

Just as there is not a standing tree without its root, so is not a destiny without its starting point. You were born because there was cohesion of two opposite sex (*father and mother*) and you were formed in the womb. Do you know what the Psalmist says about that?

> *"Behold, I was shapen in iniquity; and in sin did my mother conceive me," (Psalms 51:5).*

As innocent as you were in your mother's womb, you were drawing life genes from her in a way related to both parents' sinful nature. Not only that: you're sharing from a world you are not yet born into by transmission of hormones unknown to common knowledge because you are human already. Destiny awaits you. And the two persons that caused your formation in the womb are not sanctified as the word of God placed human race.

> *"For all have sinned, and come short of the glory of God." (Romans 3:23).*

The veil of destiny begins from this point. You joined the world of the living from parents already predestined, and they're on ground to start your upbringing on earth where caution stands in between righteous and unrighteous decisions. What followed predetermined your destiny. Did they lived together to nurture you? Or were they parted by death of one or both thereafter you were born? Or were they separated? And who were they as people on earth even if they lived together to nurture you? Why were you born by these ones? Or what purpose God has for you to be borne through these ones? What environment were you borne into? Or what influences you acquired where you were bred? All these and many other factors had predetermined one's destiny.

Then you grew to know between good and evil deeds irresistibly; and you are currently bound to choices which you're making on selfish priorities: whether they offer good virtues or not have not a rethink from you. And a self-structured world is formed wherewith you're bound to experience all occurrences of its providence. This is your destiny... where there are virtues in what you have given yourself to be, and also where there are no virtues, you will draw consequences from what you are into in your lifetime. A side of the coin of destiny! uhn?

The intricacy of destinies will lead us to the pristine giftedness inherent in some people – those who came to life endowed with supernatural skills whom challenges of destiny will contend with to debase whatever talents they are endowed with; and also considering that the *life-structure* of a man is like a parcel of land where spiritual forces plant their good and evil. Naturally, one's *life-structure* is open to his destiny: if he or she does not suffer attacks, he or she gains blessings irrespective of his inherent pristine gifts or talents. But there are gifts that engender destiny of positiveness: for *"a man's gift maketh room for him, and bringeth him before great men,"* (Proverbs 18:16)

Get this right. One's destiny is not protected from ugly realities planted by evil forces which in manifestation will predetermine what befalls a person even if he or she was privileged with inherent endowments which we claimed to be

95

pristine gifts or talents, (Read Ephesians 6:12-18). Take a deep breath! You're locked in a world of omens like a boat in troubled waters! Your *life-structure* in the hand of your destiny deserves a divine help. And God's resuscitating prophecies are constant being his words, but one's foundation may have been his or her own destiny too.

We have people who are tied to false deities and have covenant of life with shrines dedicated to principalities and powers. Somehow, they are linked with such deities by ancestral or lineage involvement in worshipping of idols. Their ancestries are cursed with a curse unto the third and fourth generations, (Deuteronomy 20:5). They bore the *mark of the beast,* (Read details of this from my book: *'VALID INTERPRETATION OF THE HOLY BIBLE – The Will Of God In All Matters').*

Some are already in the Church of God and not doing well because of ancestral curse and also because they are not fervent in their relationship with God. This is destiny inherited from descents' foundation.

> *"If the foundations be destroyed, what can the righteous do? The LORD is in his holy temple, the LORD's throne is in heaven: his eyes behold, his eyelids try, the children of men," (Psalms 11:3-4).*

Many of such people having the spell of ancestral rejection overshadowing them lack the inspiring spirits to seek a relationship with their Creator, and they live on in damnation under a destiny inherited from the platforms of abomination. And when the Lord's welcoming embrace is ignored or not pursued with enthusiasm, there be unto such persons a strangulating destiny.

> *"O LORD, the hope of Israel, all that forsake thee shall be ashamed, and they that depart from me shall be written in the earth, because they have forsaken the LORD, the fountain of living waters," (Jeremiah 17:13).*

96

The second phase of the veil of destiny starts from when one hardens his heart against the voice of the Lord, (Read Hebrews 3:7-15). What happened to you in time of ignorance may be synthesis, but what happened to you after you have heard of your Creator's experience with human race will depend on what you judged of yourself with him; whether you want God in your life or you don't. Gloomy destiny becomes engulfing where the Almighty is ignored in one's lifetime. Our Lord Jesus Christ unveiled destiny as a yoke which many have not understood what he meant, saying:

> *"Come unto me, all ye that labour and are heavy laden and I will give you rest. Take my yoke upon you, and learn of me; for I am meek and lowly in heart: and ye shall find rest unto your souls. For my yoke is easy, and my burden is light," (Matthew 11:28-30).*

Do agree to this: that we are brought forth into an omened world of supernatural forces beyond our ruling instincts. And we are susceptible to powers which our initiatives cannot undermine their supremacy over humans' attitudes and desires when we live out our time on earth. If not for God's longsuffering grace many without a relationship with the Almighty Jehovah would've resigned to a strangulating destinies because of powers meddling with their aspirations, even if they are gifted.

Satanic forces' meddling exploits predetermine what the living individuals yield to in passing the day; and because the soul of man is susceptible to spiritual influences we are doomed in self-will and unless one allows God's intervention by His words he or she will have to endure what his or her destiny offers. Because the soul of man will ever be vulnerable, the Psalmist had said:

> *"He that dwelleth in the secret place of the most High shall abide under the shadow of the Almighty... Surely he shall deliver thee from the snare of the fowler, and from the noisome pestilence. He shall cover thee with*

his feathers, and under his wings shalt thou trust: his truth shall be thy shield and buckler…

"Thou shalt not be afraid for the terror by night; nor for the arrow that flieth by day; nor for the pestilence that walketh in darkness; nor for the destruction that wasteth at noonday…For he shall give his angels charge over thee, to keep thee in all thy ways. They shall bear thee up in their hands, lest thou dash thy foot against a stone…*" (Psalms 91).*

Prophet Isaiah and the Psalmist considering what destiny caused the people of God to experience in the hand of their enemies, they individually spoke of God's help.

"And it shall come to pass in that day, that his burden shall be taken away from off thy shoulder, and his yoke from off thy neck, and the yoke shall be destroyed because of the anointing," (Isaiah 10:27).

"He sent his word, and healed them, and delivered them from their destructions," (Psalms 107:20).

Satan's formations in their realms around the world effect attacks within the confine of one's destiny to afflict and to debase the excellence in him or her. Then there is wisdom in identifying with the Almighty while we live on earth because of witches and wizards and occultists, (Read Proverbs 4:11-16). He will save you! Therefore, take these steps to allow your destiny exhibits transforming changes. It's never too late to seek the LORD God. These steps will positively affect your hopefulness to live a profiting and safe life on earth of men and supernatural forces.

1. Think on Repentance:

Repentance has been a resounding word often passed to sinners and not really much again. Is that what you're thinking? It is more than that in this matter. Many have never wanted to be addressed as sinners though the clumsiness of their destinies is impeding them in all things.

Repentance here is simply requesting that you should reverse from your first choice route in life to trail a safer route. In other words; you are aware that you believe entirely in your own ways and not the ways of the Lord. Even if you're in his kingdom being called a Christian, yet, your self-will overrides the precepts of the Lord. And supposing you're not yet a believer in Christ, you need to reverse also: for your repentance shall make your destiny to exhibit divined changes.

God was speaking through Jeremiah his prophet that his people had forsaken him, their God: and that his fear was no more in them; and God was sore bitter about these acts which he called 'two evils,' because they had forsaken him and by wayward attitude sought other mediums in search for solution. His bitterness was that he planted them as nobles and wholly a right seed, but then they turned themselves into the degenerated plant in their own ways, worshipping idols which tell they no longer saw Him as their Creator. Hear the two evils.

> "For my people have committed two evils; they have forsaken me the fountain of living waters, and hewed them out cisterns, broken cisterns, that can hold no water...
>
> "Thine own wickedness shall correct thee, and thy backslidings shall reprove thee: know therefore and see that it is an evil thing and bitter, that thou hast forsaken the LORD thy God, and that my fear is not in thee, saith the LORD God of hosts," (**Read Jeremiah 2:13-23**).

In this case, what was God expectation? Here it is! If any man may desire to experience a redefined destiny deserving God's intervention, he or she should firstly repent of his self-structured lifestyles and seek a relationship with Him. God considers forsaking him as wickedness. And what do you think of that? Then, Isaiah had never ceased portraying the consequences.

> *"Behold, I and the children whom the LORD hath given me are for signs and wonders in Israel from the LORD of hosts, which dwelleth in mount Zion…*

> *"And when they shall say unto you, Seek unto them that have familiar spirits, and unto wizards that peep, and that mutter: should not a people seek unto their God? for the living to the dead? To the law and to the testimony: if they speak not according to this word, it is because there is no light in them…*

> *"And they shall pass through it, hardly bestead and hungry: and it shall come to pass, that when they shall be hungry, they shall fret themselves, and curse their king and their God, and look upward. And they shall look unto the earth; and behold trouble and darkness, dimness of anguish; and they shall be driven to darkness," (Isaiah 8:18-22).*

These verses expressly divulged what a destiny brings forth when a nation, or a man even in togetherness with his household have a relationship with God, and when they ignored a relationship with their Creator – all being unequal.

> *"And the LORD said, Shall I hide from Abraham that thing which I do; seeing that Abraham shall surely become a great and mighty nation, and all the nations of the earth shall be blessed in him? **For I know him, that he will command his children and his household after him, and they shall keep the way of the LORD**, to do justice and judgment; **that the LORD may bring upon Abraham that which he hath spoken of him**," (Genesis 18:17-19).*

100

Therefore, your repentance should firstly be gingered toward having unquestionable relationship with your creator who will by himself structure out a destiny for you in your lifetime preserved by his prophecies. Likewise, for a whole nation as people, repentance works. Our Lord Jesus Christ considering the manner people sought after their daily resources had said:

"Therefore take no thought, saying, What shall we eat? or, What shall we drink? or, Wherewithal shall we be clothed? (For after all these things do the Gentiles seek:) for your heavenly Father knoweth that ye have need of all these things...

"But seek ye first the kingdom of God, and his righteousness; and all these things shall be added unto you. Take therefore no thought for the morrow: for the morrow shall take thought for the things of itself. Sufficient unto the day is the evil thereof," (Matthew 6:31-34).

There is wisdom in these verses, I guess you know. What led people away from God until now is their cravings that they can achieve all their heart desires on their own strength, but *"by strength shall no man prevail,"* (Read 1 Samuel 2:1-10). This was written because of destiny – a clumsy roadway!

Thereafter, repentance of moral sinfulness should follow. Your local church shall put you through on any area you need absolute repentance. And your destiny shall bless you indeed like Jabez whose prayer was granted, (1 Chronicles 4:9-10).

A nation is not excluded in this: for many nations are on a clumsy roadway even now because of their ways toward their Maker. What a world of men? Altars of wickedness surround them about as they might have adjudged considering their main religions, and not a prince or a king has boldness to break them down. But let every religion facet be a nation, no matter how small a community they are since there must be freedom of religion and let their ways judge them before the Almighty. Could this pattern ever happen considering the meshing of diverse religions that underlies all nations? God help us!

> *"And I scattered them among the heathen, and they were dispersed through the countries: according to their way and according to their doings I judged them," (Ezekiel 36:19).*

> *"We looked for peace, but no good came; and for a time of health, and behold trouble!" (Jeremiah 8:15).*

For the nations of men in this wise shall experience their destinies in their own ways without a multi-religion's tribes amalgamation which to date have caused men a lot of calamities across the global world. The altars of religions definitely would come up with their destinies in the world of men. It happened in the days of the biblical kings. Nations were understood by single altar and not multi-religions. Humans' destinies are in their hands. If strangers may therefore dwell in the nation of single altar religion, let them practice their religions in isolation not being nationally accepted: for God knows who is who. And gods adduce destinies in their kinds to their worshippers which affect their attitude to life. Then, what next after repentance?

2. Think on Obedience:

To whom honour is due, to him also obedience is due; and to whom obedience is due, to him also one can believe.

To obey is not weakness, but to disobey whom you believe on is evidence of weakness unnoticed. In prompting your destiny to exhibit divined changes, your obedience to the Almighty and spiritual leaders should be irresistible act as you journey on in life. The Prophet of Israel, Samuel, rebuked King Saul and said:

> *"Wherefore then didst thou not obey the voice of the LORD, but didst fly upon the spoil, and didst evil in the sight of the LORD? ...and Samuel said, Hath the LORD as great delight in burnt offerings and*

sacrifices, as in obeying the voice of the LORD? Behold, to obey is better than sacrifice, and to hearken than the fat of rams...

"For rebellion is as the sin of witchcraft, and stubbornness is as iniquity and idolatry. Because thou hast rejected the word of the LORD, he hath also rejected thee from being king," (Read 1 Samuel 15:1-31).

Then, Isaiah said more clearly:

"If ye be willing and obedient, ye shall eat the good of the land: but if ye refuse and rebel, ye shall be devoured with the sword: for the mouth of the LORD hath spoken it," (Isaiah 1:19-20).

Hear me O humans: disobedience to supernatural beings belies woes drawn from ugly destinies that men experience while they live. Not just God in this, but even evil deities which men had dedicated themselves too, knowingly and unknowingly. Whereas, God is merciful where righteousness is pursued, other evil deities would take a pound of flesh for disobedience to their shrines. And *life-structure* as open as it has ever been wherewith supernatural forces sow their good and evil would exhibit suffocating destiny changes when obedience to evil deities fails, unless one runs into the shelter of the Almighty. Then, I say quit and run away from indulgences with occult realms and be saved under the shadow of the Almighty. Do a rethink and quit also from your self-structured world and let God come in.

"Truth shall spring out of the earth; and righteousness shall look down from heaven," (Psalms 85:11).

Now, obedience to God is also tied to what we obey to do or not to do under our spiritual leaders. And Jehoshaphat stood in the midst of the people of God and said:

"...hear me, O Judah, and ye inhabitants of Jerusalem; Believe in the LORD your God, so shall ye be established; believe his prophets, so shall ye prosper," *(2 Chronicles 20:20).*

To whom one can believe, to him obedience is due. And this includes your spiritual leaders – pastors, apostles, prophets, teachers, evangelists, deacons and deaconesses, etc., of your local church. Irrespective of their size or prominence, you have to obey them. Destinies would exhibit changes positively or negatively depending on the side you choose; whether to obey or disobey them that have the rule over you. Repentance without obedience is hypocrisy. You don't say that you have given your life to God to think of disobeying his anointed prophets and other leaders in his vineyard: because through his prophets or leaders God reaches his people.

"Remember them which have the rule over you, who have spoken unto you the word of God: whose faith follow, considering the end of their conversation... Obey them that have the rule over you, and submit yourselves: for they watch for your souls, as they that must give account, that they may do it with joy, and not with grief: for that is unprofitable for you," (Hebrews 13:7, 17).

"Let every soul be subject unto the higher powers. For there is no power but of God: the powers that be are ordained of God. Whosoever therefore resisteth the power, resisteth the ordinance of God: and they that resist shall receive to themselves damnation," (Romans 13:1-2).

Disobedience can arise because of one's stubbornness or because of one has given himself to diverse and strange doctrines. Many Christians are extremely desperate when inordinate passions are lifted after earthly things. In this, some are failing to see reason to obey what their local pastors or leaders have directed them to observe, especially regarding certain spiritual directives. God is not the author of confusion and he will not hold you responsible for the inequality in spiritual standards of your spiritual leader compared to others if there be any; neither will he approve your desperate passions for earthly things. Faith is what God wants to see in you and not what you've given yourself to achieve from diverse and strange doctrines. So, disobedience is not excusable except that one's own pastor deviates from biblically acceptable directives.

"Be not carried about with divers and strange doctrines. For it is a good thing that the heart be established with grace, not with meats, which have not profited them that have been occupied therein," (Hebrews 13:9).

Some Christians quit their local churches and relocate as though they have rights to do so when their disobedience had ruined their relationship with the pastors they have been with. You can't do that! No! Your destiny exhibits changes for just that. How sure you are that God approved your relocation? It may not be a problem to relocate for reasons cut out for yourself, but a big problem that draws damnation when you did it after disobedient acts toward God or your local church leaders. You have more of a troubled destiny than ever. Consider this biblical proverb.

"As a bird that wandereth from her nest, so is a man that wandereth from his place," (Proverbs 27:8).

The veil of destiny! This bird that wandered away from her nest would suffer, or it might even lose its life overnight. So is a man who also wandered from his place in a local church as a result of disobedience crises.

3. Think on Service to God:

The first encounter of our Lord Jesus Christ with Saul, who is the Apostle Paul, was negotiated on ground of asking the Lord Jesus a question for service to Him.

"And he trembling and astonished said, Lord, what wilt thou have me to do? And the Lord said unto him, Arise, and go into the city, and it shall be told thee what thou must do," (Acts 9:6).

And Saul's destiny exhibited a sudden change. His world experienced astounding fame instead of his earlier horrific popularity. Service to God should not necessarily be seen as becoming an apostle, or occupying other ministerial offices in your local church but to become a co-labourer in his vineyard sets you off for his service.

"If any man serve me, let him follow me; and where I am, there shall also my servant be: if any man serve me, him will my Father honour," (John12:26).

The honour earned from our heavenly Father exceeds the honour earned from our earthly priorities. Those who had earned heavenly honour did not earn it out of nonchalance and slothfulness. They yielded their soul, mind, heart and strength to earn it. They laboured to get approval in the sight of God, (Isaiah 43:4). Many have set their pace ahead of others in service to the Almighty when they believe to the saving of their souls; exercising patience even in the face of tribulation.

"Not boasting of things without our measure, that is, of other men's labours; but having hope, when your faith is increased, that we shall be enlarged by you according to our rule abundantly, to preach the gospel in the regions beyond you, and not to boast in another man's line of things made ready to our hand...

"But he that glorieth, let him glory in the Lord. For not he that commendeth himself is approved, but whom the Lord commendeth," (2 Corinthians 10:15-18)

Apostle Paul had concord for selfless service thus saying: *"I have planted, Apollos watered; but God gave the increase... for we are labourers together with God: ye are God's husbandry, ye are God's building," (1 Corinthians 3:6, 9).*

All of us have assignments in our hands to prove our talents in the kingdom. Our Lord Jesus said we can only be his disciples when we bear much fruit and that our God is glorified when we achieve that, (John 15:8). Service to God is sowing our time, effort, and substance as necessary as we also care for our self-service as our necessities. Apostle Paul enjoined for team work saying:

> *"For as we have many members in one body, and all members have not the same office: so we, being many, are one body in Christ, and every one members one of another...*

> *"Having then gifts differing according to the grace that is given to us, whether prophecy, let us prophesy according to the proportion of faith; or ministry, let us wait on our ministering: or he that teacheth, on teaching; or he that exhorteth, on exhortation: he that giveth, let him do it with simplicity; he that ruleth, with diligence; he that sheweth mercy, with cheerfulness...*

> *"Not slothful in business; fervent in spirit; serving the Lord; rejoicing in hope; patient in tribulation; continuing instant in prayer; distributing to the necessity of saints; given to hospitality,"* **(Read Romans 12:4-13**).

There are people who have chosen to hold back their service to God: not that they are without the resourcefulness to do service to God, but that they are self-centred individuals. Job had some clues to their wilful decisions to abstain from service to God.

"Therefore they say unto God, Depart from us; for we desire not the knowledge of thy ways. What is the Almighty that we should serve him? and what profit should we have, if we pray unto him. Lo, their good is not in their hand: the counsel of the wicked is far from me," (Job 21:14-16).

Don't be like them: for they have no reflex to what their destinies will cause them. Oh, wise Job! He counted himself out from applying the folly of the fools. His latter days were better than the former since his destiny exhibited divined changes in the hand of God, (Job 42:1-17). The Psalmist said:

"The righteous shall flourish like the palm tree: he shall grow like a cedar in Lebanon. Those that be planted in the house of the LORD shall flourish in the courts of our God. They shall still bring forth fruit in old age; they shall be fat and flourishing; to shew that the LORD is upright: he is my rock, and there is no unrighteousness in him," (Psalms 92:12-15).

What? As for me, I drive my destiny under the directives God's word has offered. Now I have a destiny I can manage under all changes. His word is a lamp to my feet and a light to my path, (Psalms 119:105). Where are you positioned? What are you seeing without his word? Job refuted his wife as a foolish woman would! What can you refute where prophecy is visible? Fate will become soft where the destiny we manage is predetermined on prophecy. Our Lord Jesus Christ took to the Cross the destiny predetermined on prophecy, (**Read Isaiah 53**).

Oh, may you draw wisdom to excel in life now that you've read this book and my God will lighten your path in the knowledge of His word. Amen!

ACKNOWLEDGEMENT

My profound gratitude to the Holy Spirit for proving His worth in my life again, this time again with insights that will endure.

Also, am grateful to my family and followers and all members of OUR GARDEN OF DELIVERANCE for their supports in all areas worth thanking God for:

And to my children: Wisdom, Promise, Covenant, and Success. They were my confidence in all divine assignments.

To God be all the Glory; and here I must appreciate my Lord Jesus Christ for his work on the Cross.

Shalom!

I'm a Gifted-healer by his grace.

For

Sure deliverance and prayer for perfect healing experience…

"Evil yoke and sickness fail by what I say to them in the name of the Lord, and I always believe the sick will receive healing as I speak the word."

God's word will heal and deliver you from destructions (Psalms 107:20).

"It's living your life out of drugs! And evil yoke also will be destroyed!" (Jeremiah 17:14-15).

CALL:

+2348034745556, +2348098745556, +2348089657685.

email:

pastordavidokoduwa@yahoo.com

Books by David O. Okoduwa

1. VALID INTERPRETATION OF THE HOLY BIBLE – The Will of God in All Matters:
   To buy log on to www.createspace.com/4997472

2. Managing a Christian World:
   To buy log on to www.createspace.com/6262367

3. 3WAYS RESOURCEFUL KNOWLEDGE OF 3PERSONALITIES:
   To buy log on to www.createspace.com/6824832

4. CRUCIAL MILESTONE IN MARITAL JOURNEY
   …attractions to make couples get their marriage right!
   To buy log on to www.createspace.com/7168911